Student Study Guide
Child Development

Student Study Guide

Child Development

An Introduction

Steven R. Yussen
University of Wisconsin
Madison

John W. Santrock
University of Texas
Dallas

Second Edition
Prepared by Gene H. Brody
University of Georgia

uıcb

Wm. C. Brown Company Publishers
Dubuque, Iowa

Contents

To the Student   *vi*

Part 1   Foundations of Development   *1*
1   Introduction to Child Development   *1*
2   Biological Foundations and Physical Growth   *22*
3   Infant Development and Early Experience   *37*
4   Learning and Development   *51*

Part 2   Cognitive Development   *62*
5   Piaget's Theory of Intellectual Development   *62*
6   Information Processing   *74*
7   Language Development   *85*
8   Intelligence and Creativity   *100*

Part 3   Social, Emotional, and Personality Development   *117*
9   The Socialization Process   *117*
10   The Family and Peers   *128*
11   Schools and Culture   *146*
12   Attachment, Independence, and the Development of the Self   *161*
13   Sexual and Moral Development   *173*
14   Problems and Disturbances in Infancy, Childhood, and Adolescence   *185*

To the Student

The purpose of this study guide is to help you understand and apply the concepts presented in *Child Development: An Introduction.* This supplementary resource is designed to facilitate both understanding and appreciation of child development, not to serve as a substitute for the text itself.

How It Is Organized

Each chapter in the study guide opens with *objectives* that clearly state what you will be able to do when you have mastered the material in the chapter. For some objectives you are expected to show that you know and understand facts and ideas related to a basic knowledge of child development (define, list, describe, identify). Other objectives require that you apply what you have learned to real-life situations (relate, compare and contrast, explain, illustrate, give examples of). Still others involve making evaluations and judgments (decide, evaluate, choose). When you can accomplish these objectives, you will have mastered the chapter.

The list of *key terms* merits careful study. It focuses on the significant terms and concepts presented in the chapter; when you fully grasp their meanings, you will have a good understanding of the chapter itself. By reviewing the terms occasionally, you will quickly add them to your child-development vocabulary.

Each *synopsis* is designed to resemble a sentence outline of the chapter that you yourself might have constructed. It is an overview of the chapter's main ideas that can be used both as a preview of the scope and organization of the chapter and as a quick review to refresh your memory or to prepare for a test. Each synopsis contains some missing terms. Once you fill in the missing terms you will have a complete summary of the chapter. The missing terms are provided in the column of each synopsis page. After you have read each chapter, cover the answers and supply the missing term or terms. Then check your answer and continue on.

The three groups of exercises that follow afford you the opportunity to evaluate your progress in mastering the concepts presented in the chapter and to apply them in activities and special projects. The groups of exercises are progressively more difficult, requiring you (1) to understand the factual information presented in the chapter and begin to see how different facts are related (Self-Review), (2) to organize facts and formulate some conclusion (Comprehension), and (3) to analyze these concepts and apply them in projects involving actual studies of children or interviews of professionals who work closely with children (Application).

Answers for the first two types of exercises are provided at the end of the chapter. For the application exercises, of course, there are no "correct" answers. Through these activities you observe the principles at work that you have mastered in theory, noting how these affect children in their natural environment. You move beyond the classroom to real-life situations and beyond the textbook to experiences that allow you to make discoveries on your own—an exciting opportunity in education. Because some of these activities require careful preparation and the cooperation of other people and agencies, you would be wise to consult with your instructor well in advance about specific activities you wish to undertake.

Using the Study Guide

Now, how are you to make the best possible use of this supplementary resource for *Child Development?* Here are a few suggestions.

As you begin a chapter, first read the objectives to find out what is expected of you. Then scan the key terms. Mark any that are unfamiliar to you or that seem likely to have specialized meanings in child development; you will want to read their definitions in the glossary (at the back of the text) and be alert to their meanings in context as you read the chapter itself. You may even want to add other terms to this list as you read. Next scan the synopsis to become acquainted with the scope and organization of the chapter, and mark areas of special interest for further reading.

In reading the chapter itself, you may find it very helpful to refer now and again to these sections in the study guide. Reread the objectives to keep yourself on track, review the key terms and their meanings to make them your own, and quickly scan the synopsis for preceding sections as you begin a new major section in the chapter to maintain the sense of the whole with which you started the chapter. Make the book your own; underline key sentences, circle significant terms, jot notes and questions about items of special interest in the margins. If you prefer not to mark your text, by all means mark your study guide—each notation makes it more valuable to you as a resource and a guide.

When you have completed the chapter, turn to the exercises in your study guide. Their purpose is to make you an active participant in the learning process through self-evaluation; they are designed to help you quickly spot the facts, concepts, or principles you have not mastered so that you can review them before being tested by your instructor.

Before You Begin

A final word about the text itself. Spend a few moments—an hour would not be too long—getting acquainted with the content and organization of *Child Development*. Read the preface, the note to the reader, the contents, the part overviews, the chapter prologues and summaries. Page through a chapter or two and note such special learning aids as the topic outline at the beginning; the marginal notes; the use of boldface type to indicate words that are defined in the glossary; the tables, charts, graphs that illustrate and summarize the findings of important research studies; the insets; the review questions; the annotated reading lists. All of these special features have been designed primarily with you in mind, to present information in a form that you can easily grasp and remember. By familiarizing yourself with them, you acquire a sense of content, form, and direction for the whole that enables you to work more effectively with each part.

Part 1 Foundations of Development

1 Introduction to Child Development

Objectives

When you have mastered the material in this chapter, you will be able to—

1. define the study of child development;
2. describe prescientific themes concerning the nature of the child;
3. define theory, and discuss the functions of theory;
4. describe Freud's and Erikson's psychoanalytic theories of development;
5. describe Piaget's cognitive-structural theory of development;
6. describe the stimulus-response model of development;
7. describe the ethological view of development;
8. describe the humanistic view of development;
9. describe three scientific methods used in the study of child development—observation, experimentation, and correlation;
10. compare and contrast longitudinal, cross-sectional, and combined longitudinal cross-sectional comparisons in the study of child development.

Key Terms

accommodation
adaptation
adolescence
anal stage
assimilation
association
autonomy vs. shame and doubt
behaviorism
cognitive-structural approach
concrete operations stage
correlation
correlation index

cross-sectional method
defense mechanisms
dependent variable
development
early childhood
ego
ego integrity vs. despair
Electra complex
empirical
equilibration
erogenous zones
ethology

experience
fixation experiment
formal operations
generativity vs. stagnation
genital stage
humanism
id
identification
identity vs. role confusion
imitation
independent variable
industry vs. inferiority
infancy
initiative vs. guilt
innate knowledge
innate responses
instinct
intimacy vs. isolation
latency stage
learning theory
longitudinal comparison
maturation
mediation
middle childhood
modeling
observation
Oedipus complex

oral stage
organization
phallic stage
physical growth
pleasure principle
preoperations stage
projection
psychoanalytic theory
quasi-experiment
randomization
reaction formation
reality principle
regression
reinforcement
reliability
repression
sensorimotor stage
standardized tests
stimulus-response association
superego
tabula rasa
tension reduction
time sampling
trust vs. mistrust
youth

Synopsis

I. What Is Development?
   A. Psychologists use the term _____ to ~ development
   refer to a pattern of forward movement or change that
   begins at _____ and continues ~ conception
   throughout the entire life span.
   B. The movement is complex, because it is often the
   product of several _____ . ~ processes
      1. _____ involves changes dictated by ~ Maturation
      the genetic blueprint we each have.
      2. Physical growth refers to the simple
      _____ in size and weight that ~ changes
      occur for each child and to the gradual
      _____ changes that can be charted ~ quantitative
      for other physical and anatomical features.

2

3. _____ constitute the broadest and   Experiences
   (in some sense) vaguest ingredient in the mix of
   development.
   a) Experiences include the child's
      _____ environment—nutrition,   biological
      drugs, medical care, and physical accidents—
      and the _____ environment—   social
      family, school, community, peers, and the
      media.
   b) Experiences can be understood in
      _____ terms or in macroscopic   microscopic
      terms.
   c) Contemporary students of development seek to
      understand the kinds of experiences that shape
      maturation and growth and the processes by
      which this _____ takes place.   interaction

II. The Child in Historical Perspective
   A. Concept of childhood
      1. Philip Aires' book *Centuries of Childhood* has
         become a classic source on this topic. He makes
         clear that our present concept of
         _____ is very recent.   childhood
      2. Throughout the ages, children in art have been
         presented as miniature _____ .   adults
      3. There were basically two stages—
         _____ and   infancy
         _____ . We might generously add   adulthood
         a third stage, _____ , a time in   preadulthood
         which children learned the ways of the grown-up
         world.
   B. Children's treatment by society
      1. Prior to the nineteenth century, many infants were
         sent away to be cared for by _____   wet
         _____ or to be placed in public   nurses
         institutions until they were old enough to make an
         _____ contribution to the family.   economic
         These substitute arrangements were so bad that
         many children were never seen again by their
         families, often dying of _____   neglect
         and malnutrition. In medieval or ancient
         times, _____ was common.   infanticide

2. For children who survived infancy,
_____ was more rampant and   abuse
there were no legal sanctions against it as there are
today.

C. Acquiring knowledge about children
1. Scholars in the past tended to focus on
philosophical debates about children that were
difficult to settle on _____ terms.   empirical
One philosophical debate concerns the origin of

_____ .   knowledge

a) According to the position of
_____ knowledge, the child is   innate
born with both knowledge about the world and
strong propensities to learn.

b) By contrast, British philosopher John Locke
suggested that at birth the child's mind is a

_____ _____ ,   blank slate
a tabula rasa.

2. The second subject for philosophical debate
concerned the moral goodness of the child and the
need for _____   moral

_____ .   training

a) The child is inherently bad, or sinful, at

_____ ,   birth

b) or the child is inherently _____   good
at birth.

D. Child development in contemporary times
1. In the past half century, we have come to view
childhood as a highly eventful and unique period of
life that lays an important _____   foundation
for the adult years.

2. Future policies for and decisions about children can
be based upon an accumulating body of knowledge
of what children are like, based in turn on
_____ evidence rather than   scientific
philosophical speculation.

III. Theories of Development
A. A scientific theory is an organized and logical set of
statements, laws, and _____ .   axioms
1. One of its functions is to describe carefully some
_____ events.   observable
2. A second function of a theory is to
_____ some observable events.   explain

3. A third function of a theory is to
_____ observable events.   predict

4. A good theory should be complete and terse. It is important for the theory to describe and explain as much as possible, yet it should satisfy this requirement with an economical use of statements and _____ .   concepts

5. A good theory should also be precise, making specific predictions about what can be expected in different situations so that the theory can be clearly proved _____ .   wrong

B. The psychoanalytic perspective
1. Psychoanalytic theory refers to the set of assumptions shared by _____   Sigmund
_____ and many followers of his   Freud
theory of development.

  a) Freud's theory stresses the biological forces that shape human destiny. One important biological force is _____ .   instinct

  b) All of development may be seen as the result of changes in the way instinctual
_____ is channeled and   energy
organized.

  c) Freud's theory claims that mental life can be divided into three different structures or parts—id, ego, and superego.

    (1) At birth the infant is dominated by
_____ impulses (id).   instinctual

      (a) These impulses operate
_____ and   unconsciously
irrationally.

      (b) The infant's search for any object to satisfy a need, without regard for its reality or need-reducing value, is referred to as the

_____   pleasure
_____ , or primary   principle
process thinking.

    (2) The infant gradually learns to distinguish between objects that are truly satisfying and those that only appear to be satisfying. This learning constitutes the beginning of the development of the _____ .   ego

(a) The ego consists of rational thoughts, perceptions, and plans to help the child cope with

_____ .   reality

(b) Much of the ego's functioning is conscious and rational, and it attempts to channel instinctual energy toward objects that will realistically satisfy needs. This orientation toward reality and need-reducing value is referred to as the

_____   reality

_____ , or secondary   principle

process thinking.

(3) The final mental system to develop is the superego, which consists of

_____ rules to guide the   moral

child's actions.

d) As the mental systems evolve, the child experiences five clearly distinguishable developmental _____ .   stages

(1) The _____ stage centers   oral

on the child's pleasure from stimulation of the oral area. This stage lasts from birth to about one year.

(2) The _____ stage lasts   anal

from two to three years of age and centers on the child's pleasure with the exercise of the anus, or eliminative activity.

(3) During the _____ stage,   phallic

which lasts from about four to six years of age, instinctual energy is focused on the genital area.

(a) During the phallic stage the Oedipal and Electra complexes erupt.

(b) The troublesome feelings associated with these complexes are

_____ , driven   repressed

from consciousness and locked away in the unconscious id.

(4) The long period of middle childhood, which lasts from about six to twelve years of age, is known as the _____ latency stage. During this stage the child concentrates on exploring the environment and mastering the vast number of intellectual skills needed for getting along in society.

(5) The last of Freud's stages of development is the _____ stage, which genital occurs from about thirteen to nineteen years of age. During this period the repression of Oedipal feelings is lifted and teenagers experience a sudden surge of interest in _____ matters. sexual

2. Several processes and mechanisms in Freud's theory, when taken collectively, help to explain _____ changes in behavior. developmental

   a) One important mechanism is tension _____ . reduction
   Freud believed that tension reduction is inherently _____ and is the pleasurable principal motivating force behind all behavior.

   b) Another mechanism for change is _____ , the incorporation identification of behavior and attitudes of another person into one's own structure of thought and action.

   c) _____ is a defense mechanism Repression defined as an anxiety-provoking thought or feeling being forced out of the consciousness into the unconscious.

   d) In _____ , an anxiety- projection provoking thought or feeling is shifted from its actual source (the child) to an external object or source.

   e) _____ _____ Reaction formation is a defense that consists of changing a troublesome thought or feeling into its opposite.

   f) When a child appears to become temporarily stuck in one stage of development, or if a child seems to backslide in development, we are seeing the related defenses of _____ and fixation _____ . regression

3. Few psychologists accept all of Freud's major theoretical concepts today. Contemporary psychoanalytic thinkers believe Freud shortchanged the importance of _____ . The   culture
theorist most responsible for changing that is

_____ _____ .   Erik Erikson

   a) Erikson's theory is particularly important because it stresses rational or _____   ego
processes; because it sensitively captures the

      _____ experience; and   adolescent
because, in its entirety, it casts a

      _____ frame of reference on   life-span
development.

   b) Erikson postulates _____   eight
stages of development, the first _____   five
of which correspond to Freud's stages.

   c) The last three stages, _____   intimacy
vs. isolation, _____ vs.   generativity
stagnation, and _____   ego
_____ vs. despair, extend   integrity
Freud's theory into adulthood.

C. The cognitive-structural perspective

  1. This perspective focuses on rational thinking processes in the child. The term

     _____ underscores the interest   cognitive
in thought and rational mental processes. The

     term _____ highlights the concern   structural
with the way in which thought is organized at different stages—hence its structure.

  2. Jean Piaget is the leading contemporary figure who holds this point of view.

   a) Piaget believes that the core of intelligence is rationality and that intelligence develops from the interplay of several hereditary and

      _____ forces.   environmental

   b) Piaget tends to be concerned with _____   how
children think rather than with what they think about or how many facts they know.

  3. Piaget claims that all children move through recognized _____ in an established   stages
sequence.

a) The _____ stage lasts from birth to about two years of age. During this time the infant develops the ability to organize and coordinate sensations and perceptions with physical movements.

sensorimotor

b) The _____ stage lasts from two to seven years of age. Despite cognitive advances during this period, there are a number of limitations or flaws in the child's thought processes. Among the major flaws are the child's egocentrism, inability to _____ , and failure to order objects in a series and classify them.

preoperational

conserve

c) During the stage of _____ operations, which lasts from seven to eleven years of age, the flaws or the preoperational stage disappears. The shift to this more perfect system of thinking is brought about by the shift from egocentrism to _____ and the child's ability to mentally pose and operate on a series of actions. However, the child relies on concrete events in order to think in this way.

concrete

relativism

d) The _____ operations stage comes into play between eleven and fourteen years of age. The most important single feature of this stage is the adolescent's ability to move beyond the world of actual, concrete experiences. The child can think _____ , using abstract propositions and make-believe or contrary-to-fact events, and test hypotheses in a deductive fashion.

formal

logically

4. Piaget uses several different _____ and explanations to explain how change occurs in children's thoughts.

processes

a) The first process responsible for change is _____ , the child's ability to interact effectively with the environment. This process is subdivided into _____ and _____ . The child tries to incorporate features of the environment into already existing ways of thinking about them

adaptation

assimilation
accommodation

9

and to incorporate new features of the
environment into his or her thinking by
modifying existing modes of thought.

    b) A second mechanism of change is
_____ . Every level of thought,   organization
from sensorimotor to formal, is organized, and
continual improvement of this organization is
an inherent part of development.

    c) _____ is a third mechanism   Equilibration
invoked to explain how a child shifts from one
stage to the next. The goal of better
organization is to reach a more lasting state of
balance in thought.

D. The stimulus-response association perspective
  1. In this view, the world of the child can be divided
into observable stimuli, observable responses, and
their interrelationships.

    a) A _____ may be any event in   stimulus
the environment associated with a response.

    b) This view maintains that behavior comes about
through the process of _____ .   learning

  2. There are at least three main learning processes.

    a) _____ is one process. When a   Association
stimulus and a response repeatedly occur
together, they eventually become linked
together in the mind of the observer.

    b) Another process is _____ . A   reinforcement
stimulus may follow a response and increase
the probability that the response will occur
again.

    c) _____ is a third process. If a   Imitation
child watches someone else do something, the
child may repeat the action if there is sufficient
incentive.

  3. _____ is seen as the accumulation   Development
of new responses through learning. Each child's
pattern of learning is different—different
associations have been learned, different responses
rewarded, and different models made available for
imitation—so each child has a unique learning
history.

4. The S-R perspective evolved in the absence of detailed information about children. As research with children caught up to theoretical ideas about S-R learning, it became clear that other concepts had to be introduced to handle the diverse facts about development.

   a) One such concept is mediation. A _____ is a cognitive event that occurs between the stimulus and the response.   **mediator**

   b) Another concept is that there are several levels of learning. Rather than view the age changes as due to mediation, some theorists prefer to postulate that learning has a building-block nature, with the different levels of rules forming a type of _____ .   **hierarchy**

5. Important advances have been made in understanding how children think in "real time" with newer approaches, but the lasting contribution of Piaget's work is that he gave us a _____ _____ of where to look and some important phenomena to look at.   **big picture**

E. Other theoretical perspectives
  1. The ethological perspective
    a) Ethology is the study of the _____ basis of behavior. The movement emerged because a number of European _____ believed that learning theories had led behavioral scientists to an almost complete neglect of the innate basis of many behaviors.   **biological**   **zoologists**

    b) Ethologists believe that certain events in the environment evoke _____ responses in various animals because the animals are programmed from birth to respond this way.   **innate**

    c) Ethologists use _____ observation and try not to interfere with the natural environment.   **naturalistic**

  2. The humanistic perspective
    a) Humanism is a cluster of attitudes about how to view children and their growth. Maslow's theory of _____ , Rogers's client-centered therapy, and Gordon's   **self-actualization**

transactional-analysis perspective are all examples of humanistic theories of development.

b) The theories seem to contain philosophical articles of _____ about humans rather than scientific laws and principles leading to testable ideas about development.   faith

   (1) _____ believe that focus should be on the uniqueness of each child, the child's global self, the child's capacity for constructive growth and creative potential, and the importance of values, attitudes, and beliefs rather than the specific interchange of social behaviors.   Humanists

   (2) Helping children and adults live more satisfying lives and have more effective interpersonal _____ is a prominent theme in humanism.   relations

IV. Child Psychology as a Scientific Enterprise
  A. Perhaps the most basic tool of any science is systematic observation.

    1. _____ observation means that the observer must be trained to look only for certain behaviors during an observation. For example, if aggression is under investigation, then only aggressive behaviors are _____ .   Systematic

     observed

    2. Most observational studies require time _____ , a procedure in which the child is observed only a portion of the time. For example, a child might be observed in alternating two-minute observe-record cycles; a two-minute observation period would be followed by a two-minute recording period.   sampling

    3. When different observers agree on what has been observed, the records are considered _____ . If the observers do not substantially agree, the observations are considered unreliable and, in effect, worthless.   reliable

4. Roger Barker developed a specialized technique of naturalistic observation called _____ psychology. With this technique a child's behavior is observed by teams of observers as the child goes about a typical day's activities.

    ecological

B. In an _____ , an attempt is made to exercise control over certain factors. Factors thought to influence or cause something are referred to as _____ variables; the experimenter attempts to manipulate these in a study. Factors that are being influenced are referred to as _____ variables; these are measured in a study.

    experiment

    independent

    dependent

  1. _____ two experimental groups is one way to discover whether the independent variables were responsible for results obtained. Another technique to determine this is known as _____ .

    Matching

    randomization

  2. Experiments that are carefully controlled are useful because they permit the experimenter to make _____ about cause-and-effect relations.

    inferences

C. One measure of association between characteristics such as height and weight is the _____ _____ .

    correlation
    index

  1. The correlation index ranges from -1.00 to $+1.00$. A negative number indicates a _____ _____ .

    negative relation

  2. A correlation alone cannot be used to support the interpretation that one event _____ another.

    causes

D. Other methods

  1. In a _____-experiment some control is exercised over one or more independent variables. The control is not perfect, however, because the independent variables were defined as part of some societal or institutional program, not as part of an experimental design, so _____ variables are often associated with those that are of interest.

    quasi

    hidden

2. Another technique is to question children directly about some facet of their lives or behavior. An interview can be especially valuable when a lot of information about a child must be obtained in a short period of time.

3. A _____ test, which is an instrument administered to hundreds or thousands of children to establish performance levels used in comparisons, can be used to compare individual children with others their own age, to match children at the same level on a characteristic, or to assess an individual child's _____ .

    standardized

    progress

E. Developmental comparisons
  1. Longitudinal Method
    a) One way to measure age-related changes in children is to test an individual child _____ over time.

    repeatedly

    b) The longitudinal method is valued because it enables researchers to observe changes unfolding in _____ children.

    individual

    c) This method is often _____ because children may withdraw from a study as a result of school and residence changes, personnel may change, and the cost in time and money may be excessive.

    impractical

  2. Cross-sectional method
    a) Groups of children of different ages are studied at about the same time, and age changes are inferred from differences among the _____ .

    groups

    b) A cross-sectional study is valued because it permits the detection of a _____ change in a fairly short period of time by testing a large number of children.

    developmental

    c) It is difficult to be sure that group patterns reflect differences between age groups because children usually grow up under different circumstances.

3. Combined longitudinal/cross-sectional method
    a) This combined approach allows the researcher to see whether the cross-sectional and longitudinal approaches both yield the same _____ of developmental change.   pattern
    b) If the two approaches yield different patterns, the cause of the _____ can sometimes be identified.   discrepancy

Exercises

Self-Review

Circle the letter of the best response.

1. Changes dictated by genetic blueprints are referred to as
    a. growth.
    b. maturation.
    c. development.
    d. biological.

2. A pattern of forward movement or change that begins at conception is known as
    a. growth.
    b. maturation.
    c. development.
    d. biological.

3. Through the middle ages, artists portrayed children as
    a. miniature adults.
    b. small children.
    c. adolescents.
    d. infants.

4. Prior to the nineteenth century, many infants were often sent away to be cared for by
    a. foster parents.
    b. grandparents.
    c. nannies.
    d. wet nurses.

5. The British philosopher John Locke suggested that at birth the child's mind is
   a. an undeveloped machine.
   b. a bundle of associations.
   c. a blank slate.
   d. governed by the pleasure principle.

6. An organized set of statements, laws, and axioms is called
   a. concept.
   b. fact.
   c. hypothesis.
   d. theory.

7. One important criteria for a good theory is that it can be
   a. proved wrong.
   b. understood.
   c. descriptive.
   d. innovative.

8. Psychoanalytic theory refers to the set of assumptions shared by
   a. Piaget.
   b. Freud.
   c. Lorenz.
   d. Rogers.

9. Freud's theory claims that mental life can be divided into three different structures or parts. These are
   a. real, ideal, and false selves.
   b. sensorimotor, concrete, and formal.
   c. id, ego, and superego.
   d. I, me, and it.

10. According to Freud, the long period of middle childhood that lasts from about six to twelve years of age is known as the
    a. genital stage.
    b. anal stage.
    c. latency stage.
    d. oral stage.

11. One of Erikson's contributions to psychoanalytic theory is that he recognized the importance of
    a. nuclear families.
    b. culture.
    c. sex.
    d. infancy.

12. The person most closely identified with the cognitive developmental perspective is
    a. Harry Harlow.
    b. Albert Bandura.
    c. Sigmund Freud.
    d. Jean Piaget.

13. According to Piaget, the stage that lasts from two to seven years of age is
    a. sensorimotor.
    b. preoperational.
    c. concrete operational.
    d. formal operations.

14. In cognitive developmental terms, adaptation is subdivided into
    a. organization and disequilibrium.
    b. assimilation and accommodation.
    c. conservation and nonconservation.
    d. hierarchical rules.

15. From the stimulus-response association perspective, development is often equated with
    a. learning.
    b. heredity.
    c. organization.
    d. equilibration.

16. The three learning processes that have received a great deal of attention are
    a. axioms, laws, and facts.
    b. id, ego, and superego.
    c. assimilation, accommodation, and equilibration.
    d. association, reinforcement, and imitation.

17. Ethologists believe that certain events in the environment evoke
    a. innate responses.
    b. reinforcements.
    c. punishments.
    d. imitation.

18. Roger Barker developed a specialized technique of naturalistic observations called
    a. environmental psychology.
    b. information processing.
    c. ecological psychology.
    d. operant psychology.

19. When different observers agree on what has been observed, the records are considered
    a. random.
    b. consistent.
    c. valid.
    d. reliable.

20. Variables that are thought to influence or cause something are
    a. independent.
    b. dependent.
    c. hidden.
    d. confounded.

Comprehension

1. The following excerpt illustrates a special technique of naturalistic observation. Read it carefully and answer the questions that follow.

> Renee requests matter-of-factly, "I want a drink of milk."
> She looks over at her mother as she says this.
> The mother walks a few steps to the refrigerator.
> She starts to pull at the refrigerator door but turns abruptly.
> She walks the few steps to where Peter is.
> She leans over and kisses him affectionately on the back of the neck.
> Peter smiles a broad smile as if really enjoying this attention.
> The mother immediately turns back to the refrigerator.
> She reaches for the refrigerator handle as she turns.
> "I want some juice," says Renee more firmly as if she has changed her mind.
> "No, there isn't any juice made," says the mother as if she is considering this. "How about milk?"
> "No," Renee insists firmly.
> "We can make some," Renee explains as if she insists that her suggestion can be followed.
> "How about chocolate milk?" asks the mother as if Renee will surely say yes to this.
> "You can make some," says Renee much more insistently, her voice rising in pitch. "You can make some," she repeats insistently.

18

M. Schoggen, "An Ecological Approach to the Study of Mother-Child Interactions" (Nashville: George Peabody College for Teachers, 1969), pp. 20.03–5,–6.

a. What is the name of the specialized technique of observation?

b. How does this technique differ from other observational techniques?

2. Descriptions of research projects that scientists interested in child development could investigate follow. Read each description carefully and below it write the name of one of the five theoretical perspectives that is the most likely to sponsor it.

a. Mother, father, and their sons are observed in a laboratory. The investigators are examining whether the father and son compete for the mother's attention when interacting with the mother at the same time.

b. A team of educational psychologists wants to determine whether the presence of certain cognitive structures is necessary to perform mathematical tasks well. Therefore, the investigators randomly sampled thirty first-graders and thirty third-graders. The children were given a test to determine whether their cognitive abilities could be classified as concrete-operational. The researchers divided the children into groups that did or did not possess concrete-operational skills. Then each child was exposed to instruction that attempted to teach a new mathematical concept.

c. Fifty third-graders and fifty sixth-graders were escorted into a television viewing room, one at a time. The children were shown one of three specially constructed television programs. The first depicted a child playing violently with some toys; the second program was like the first, except that two children were playing violently with the toys. The third program depicted some nonviolent documentary material. After the children had viewed one of these revised episodes, they were escorted to another room, where their play behavior was observed and the presence or absence of violence was recorded. This study addresses whether violence can be learned through imitation.

d. Thirty preschool children were observed in the school playground during recess. The researchers were interested in whether or not children respond as other mammals do when they want to indicate to an aggressor that they have lost a fight. For example, many mammals lie on their backs and expose their stomachs when they yield to an opponent. If the preschoolers do respond in a similar manner, then these researchers would speculate that this behavior could be innately determined.

e. A team of researchers sought to determine whether parents who attended parent training classes were not only effective parents but reared children who had well-integrated global self-concepts. The parent-child interactions of those who went through the parent training program were compared with the parent-child interactions of those who did not take part in the program.

Application

Now you have a chance to be an amateur child psychologist. You are to observe a preschool child two times, each time for forty minutes. Suppose that you are a behavioristic child psychologist and one of your major concerns is how a child's environment teaches the child new behaviors. In other words, you are interested in what behaviors receive reinforcement and who the reinforcing agents are. Carefully observe a preschool child for five minutes. Record each behavior that receives reinforcement. Also record what kinds of reinforcers (e.g., smiles, hugs, snacks, access to play material) the child received and who provided the reinforcement. After completing your observation, answer the following questions.

1. What different behaviors received reinforcement?

2. What different kinds of reinforcers did the child receive?

3. Who provided the reinforcers to the child?

4. From your observation, what did you learn about how children receive reinforcement?

Answers

1. b	11. b
2. c	12. d
3. a	13. b
4. d	14. b
5. c	15. a
6. d	16. d
7. a	17. a
8. b	18. c
9. c	19. d
10. c	20. a

Comprehension

1. a. Ecological psychology; b. In this technique, a child's behavior is observed all day long by teams of observers.
2. a. psychoanalytic; b. cognitive-structural; c. stimulus-response; d. ethological; e. humanistic.

---

2 Biological Foundations and Physical Growth

Objectives

When you have mastered the material in this chapter, you will be able to—

1. identify the basic principles of heredity and genetics;
2. describe the structure of the DNA molecule;
3. explain the transmission of characteristics;
4. discuss the interaction of heredity and environment in determining the characteristics of individuals;
5. describe the contribution of heredity to different characteristics of individuals;
6. describe the determination of maleness and femaleness;
7. describe conception and prenatal development;
8. list and discuss the capabilities of the newborn infant;
9. discuss physical growth of the child following birth;
10. describe the function of each part of the brain.

Key Terms

age of viability
androgens
association areas
axon
brain
central nervous system
cephalo-caudal growth
cerebellum
cerebrum
chromosomes
conception
consanguinity study
continuum of indirectness
DNA
dominant code
dorsal root
Down's syndrome
embryonic period
estrogens
fallopian tube
fetal alcohol syndrome
fetal period
general hereditary code
genes
genotype
germinal period
heritability quotient
inbreeding

medulla oblongata
Mendel's laws
mental retardation
midbrain
mitosis
motor cortex
myelin sheath
neuron
occipital lobe
ovum
parietal lobe
phenotype
PKU syndrome
placenta
polygenetically
pons
prenatal period
recessive code
selective breeding
sensory cortex
specific hereditary code
sperm cell
spinal cord
temporal lobe
thalamus
umbilical cord
ventral root

Synopsis

I. Introduction

  A. The story of human development begins at conception when a single male _____ fertilizes the female _____ .

    sperm
    ovum

  B. The prebirth span is called the _____ period.

    prenatal

II. Heredity

  A. Each of us has two hereditary codes.

    1. The _____ hereditary code that all humans share accounts for physical and psychological sameness.

      general

2. The _____ hereditary code   specific
   accounts for the uniqueness of each person.
B. The process of development is directed by genetic
   material contained in the _____ of   nucleus
   each original cell—the sperm and egg.
   1. Each nucleus contains twenty-three
      _____ . A chromosome is a long,   chromosomes
      complex, chainlike structure containing many
      thousands of _____ .   genes
   2. These two cells, sometimes called reproductive or
      _____ cells, are the only ones we   germ
      possess that contain precisely twenty-three
      chromosomes. They combine to give forty-six
      chromosomes.
   3. As the _____ egg divides and   fertilized
      redivides over the next several weeks, a process
      called _____ , each new cell has a mitosis
      replica of the same forty-six chromosomes arranged
      in the same way.
   4. A gene was thought to be the smallest building
      block in the process of hereditary transmission;
      actually it is a complex _____ .   molecule
      The structure of this molecule is known as
      _____ and is arranged as if in a   DNA
      spiral staircase—the _____   double
      _____ .   helix
C. The unique arrangement and characteristics of the
   chromosomes and genes inherited make each person
   unique.
   1. The total constellation of chromosomes and genes
      and their unique configuration in an individual is
      referred to as a person's _____ .   genotype
   2. All the observable and measurable characteristics of
      an individual are referred to as the person's
      _____ . These characteristics may   phenotype
      be physical or psychological.
   3. Identical phenotypical characteristics may be
      produced by different _____ .   genotypes
D. In the nineteenth century Gregor Mendel uncovered
   some basic principles, now known as
   _____ _____ , that   Mendel's laws
   explain what happens when genes are combined.

1. For each characteristic there are two
_____ (one from each parent) that   genes
may carry identical codes or different codes.
2. Some gene codes are _____ and   dominant
others recessive. The recessive feature will appear
only if two recessive genes, one from each parent,
combine.

E. Some characteristics, such as color blindness, depend on
genes carried in the twenty-third chromosome pair—the
pair that also determines the _____ of   sex
the offspring—with the result that these characteristics
are more or less likely to occur in members of one sex.

F. Genetic determination is often more complicated than
one might think.
1. Dominance and recessiveness are not
_____ ; for some characteristics   absolute
they are relative, resulting in qualitative mixtures.
2. Few characteristics are determined by the action of
single gene pairs; most are actually determined by
the _____ of many different genes   interaction
in the chromosomes. These traits are described as
_____ determined.   polygenically
3. Virtually all _____ characteristics   psychological
are the result of an interaction between the child's
inherited code and environmental influences.

G. Anne Anastasi developed a continuum of influence of
heredity on development. She referred to it as the

_____ _____   continuum of
_____ .   indirectness

H. There are several different strategies for examining the
influence of _____ in developmental   heredity
processes.
1. One is to compare identical _____   twins
with nonidentical _____ .   twins
2. In a _____ study, known   consanguinity
relations, such as fathers and sons, siblings, and
cousins, are compared with randomly paired
individuals who are unrelated.
3. It is possible to look at groups who are related
genetically but whose _____ vary.   environments
Twins and siblings, for example, are sometimes
reared by different families as a result of divorce or
death of their parents.

4. Because all methods employed with humans are of a _____ or quasi-experimental nature due to the ethical questions involved when attempts are made to manipulate human genetics, much research has been done on lower animals.   correlational

   a) In _____ breeding experiments animals are mated over successive generations on the basis of a similar specific characteristic.   selective

   b) In _____ experiments males and females from the same parents are mated.   inbreeding

I. Our ability to control other important variables is often weak and so it is difficult to say that a specific characteristic is determined by heredity. Estimates of the heritability of a particular characteristic are often computed with a standard _____ _____ that is between 0 and + 1.00.   heritability quotient

J. There are a number of _____ disorders that create mental retardation. Genetic transmission may easily be traced to the _____ features of retardation.   genetic

     secondary

  1. In amaurotic idiocy, blindness and physical paralysis result from impairments to the _____ and nervous system.   brain

  2. In the _____ syndrome the problem resides in a genetic code that fails to produce an enzyme necessary for metabolism.   PKU

  3. In _____ _____ the child has an extra chromosome.   Down's syndrome

III. Physical Development and Maturation

  A. Important changes take place prior to birth.

    1. Life begins when a single sperm cell from the male unites with the ovum (egg) in the female's _____ _____ in a process called fertilization or conception. It normally occurs at the midpoint of the woman's _____ _____ .   Fallopian tube

     menstrual cycle

    2. The _____ period is two weeks after conception. Two major developments occur during this time.   germinal

a) One is continued cell _____ .   division
Prior to each division the _____   chromosome
pairs double and then split, with each new cell
retaining a replica of the original twenty-three
pairs of chromosomes.

b) A second event is the firm attachment to the
wall of the _____ .   uterus

3. The _____ period lasts from about   embryonic
two to eight weeks.

a) During this period a primitive
_____ form takes shape.   human

b) The part of the embryo attached to the uterine
wall becomes the _____ , the   placenta
meeting ground for the circulatory system of
both embryo and mother.

c) The _____ _____   umbilical cord
transports waste substances from the embryo to
the placental barrier; the cord also has
membranes that allow for the passage of only
certain substances.

d) By the end of this period the _____   embryo
is about one-inch long and weighs about half an
ounce.

4. The _____ period lasts from about   fetal
eight weeks until birth—a total of seven months in
full-term babies.

a) By _____ weeks of age the   twelve
fetus is about three inches long, weighs
approximately one ounce, has begun to move
vigorously, and has a number of well-
differentiated physical and anatomical features.

b) By the end of the fourth month the fetus is
about six inches long, weighs four ounces, has a
growth spurt in the _____   lower
part of the body, and has a number of
prenatal _____ strong enough   reflexes
to be felt by the mother.

c) By the end of the fifth month, the
_____ is about a foot long,   fetus
weighs about a pound, and begins to form skin
structures, fingernails, and toenails.

    d) By the end of the sixth month the fetus is
about fourteen inches long, weighs about two
pounds, has completely formed eyes and
eyelids, has a fine layer of _____ ,   hair
and exhibits a grasping reflex.

    e) By the end of the seventh month the fetus is
about sixteen inches long, weighs about three
pounds, and has reached the age of

      _____ .   viability

    f) During the eighth and ninth months the fetus
grows longer and there is a substantial

      _____ _____ .   weight gain
At birth, the average American baby is twenty
inches long and weighs seven pounds.

B. There are a variety of environmental influences on
prenatal development.

  1. The mother's general _____ is   health
important.

    a) German _____ contracted by   measles
the mother during the first three months of
pregnancy can cause mental retardation in the
infant.

    b) _____ in the mother causes   Diabetes
circulatory and breathing problems in infants.

  2. Nutrition is also important.

    a) Children born to mothers with poor diets are
more likely to contract _____   disease
during infancy.

    b) Some investigators believe that malnutrition is
linked to mental _____   retardation
because of the importance of
_____ in brain development.   protein

  3. Several studies have shown that the woman's
emotional temperament is also important.

    a) Severe _____ may cause   depression
hormones that increase activity level to be
released in the infant.

    b) There is also some belief that low-level
(depressed) activity in newborns may be related
to _____ during pregnancy.   stress

4. Physicians are cautious about the use of
_____ by pregnant women because   drugs
they can cause problems for the infant such as
physical malformation, addiction, depressed
breathing, and lethargy.

C. There are two periods of greatest general growth—
infancy, especially the first year, and
_____ . Curves have been developed to   adolescence
describe growth patterns.

  1. The _____ and head have only   brain
one period of sharp change, which is from birth to
approximately age three.

  2. A truism in the study of growth is that change
occurs in a _____ pattern, from   cephalo-caudal
top to bottom.

  3. Rapid change in the _____ system   reproductive
occurs during adolescence.

  4. Growth in _____ tissues is fairly   lymphnoid
uniform from birth to about six years.

  5. A variety of factors influence growth curves.

    a) Growth is often _____ seeking   target
or self-stabilizing. In cases where growth has
been stunted by disease or poor
_____ , the individual's growth   nutrition
often catches up with its original path after the
negative conditions have been removed.

    b) _____ _____   Maturity gradients
exist so that, for example, the head is always
more developmentally advanced than the trunk.

    c) _____ _____   Feedback regulation
entails the adaptation of biological structures to
feedback.

    d) Frish and Revelle believe that the body has
built-in sensors to detect when a certain
_____ _____   body mass
is reached.

IV. The Central Nervous System

A. The average adult brain is approximately the size of a
clenched _____ and weighs about   fist
three pounds.

B. The _____ _____ is   spinal cord
the cylinderlike part of the central nervous system that
occupies the upper portion of the column of vertebra
within the spinal column and serves as the passageway
for numerous nerve _____ and nerve   fibers
_____ .   roots

   1. The _____ pathway contains the   sensory
      nerve fibers that transmit stimulation initially
      received from various sensory organs.
   2. The _____ pathway transmits   motor
      impulses from the brain and spinal cord to various
      parts of the body.

C. Major structures of the brain have different functions.
   1. The _____ _____   medulla oblongata
      is the structure sitting atop the spinal cord that
      contains a number of neurons that help regulate the
      control of breathing and _____   blood
      _____ .   pressure

   2. The _____ is just above the   pons
      medulla oblongata and consists of a number of
      fibers connecting the two hemispheres of the
      cerebellum and a separate set of fibers connecting
      the medulla with the cerebrum.
   3. The _____ is located above the   cerebellum
      lower part of the brain stem and consists of a
      center section and two lateral hemispheres. It is
      critical in coordinating movement with
      _____ .   sensation
   4. The _____ connects the pons and   midbrain
      cerebellum with the cerebrum. It conveys the
      sensations of _____ , heat, and   pain
      cold to areas in the thalamus and transmits neural
      messages that control reflex movements such as
      balance and bodily posture.
   5. The _____ _____   cerebral hemispheres
      are perhaps the most important structures of our
      human brains.
      a) Each hemisphere can be divided into areas, or
         lobes.
         (1) Within the _____ lobe is   temporal
            a region that controls auditory perception.
         (2) The _____ lobe is   occipital
            involved in visual perception.

(3) The _____ lobe is   parietal
    involved in speech and language.
b) As a whole the cerebral hemisphere can be
   divided into specific regions.
    (1) The _____ cortex receives   sensory
        inputs from bodily sensations directly from
        the thalamus (primary sensory cortex) and
        also from other areas in the sensory cortex
        (thus, secondary sensory cortex).
    (2) The _____ cortex is the   motor
        origin of signals transmitted to specific
        parts of the body.
    (3) There are _____ areas   association
        throughout a large portion of the rest of
        the cerebral cortex that are responsible for
        integrating and coordinating sensation and
        action pathways, storing
        _____ , and allowing us to   memories
        perform a number of intellectual
        operations.
D. Development of the brain and central nervous system
   begins shortly after _____ .   conception
   1. Within two weeks after fertilization a slender,
      tubelike structure becomes differentiated from the
      other _____ of the body.   cells
   2. Following birth, there is very rapid growth of the
      _____ , but it is not until two   brain
      years that the brain takes on the proportions it will
      have at maturity.
   3. At birth, we have all the _____   neurons
      that will ever exist. These cells responsible for
      transmitting _____ to and from   information
      the brain will grow in overall size with maturation.
   4. _____ is the process that largely   Myelination
      accounts for increases in the speed of transmission
      of neural messages.
      a) On the _____ of many cells   axons
         there is a soft, white, fatty substance called
         _____ , surrounded by an   myelin
         encasement called a myelin sheath.
      b) Even at _____ , not all   maturity
         neurons are myelinated.

c) Myelination affects the _____ speed
with which impulses are conducted along the
axon.

d) There appears to be an _____ order
in which neurons are myelinated, with neurons
serving common functions myelinated at
approximately the same point in time.

Exercises

Self-Review

Circle the letter of the best response.

1. The biochemical agents that carry the biological code each of
   us inherits are known as
   a. genotypes and phenotypes.
   b. genes and chromosomes.
   c. enzymes.
   d. catalysts.

2. Another name for cell division is
   a. albinism.
   b. consanguinity.
   c. recessive code.
   d. mitosis.

3. "Spiral staircase" and "double helix" describe
   a. steroids.
   b. amino acids.
   c. DNA molecules.
   d. enzymes.

4. The total constellation of chromosomes and genes and their
   unique configuration in an individual are referred to as the
   a. genotype.
   b. phenotype.
   c. potential quotient.
   d. heritability quotient.

5. All the observable and measurable characteristics of an individual are referred to as the
   a. genotype.
   b. phenotype.
   c. personality.
   d. disposition.

6. A recessive feature will appear only when
    a. one dominant gene and one recessive gene combine.
    b. dominant genes are transmitted across several generations in a family.
    c. two recessive genes combine.
    d. it occurs on the Y chromosome.

7. The mathematical technique that allows us to estimate the amount of variation in a hereditary characteristic is called the
    a. continuum of indirectness.
    b. heritability quotient.
    c. biological code.
    d. genotype.

8. A consanguinity study compares
    a. known relations with randomly paired individuals.
    b. known relations with nonrandomly paired individuals.
    c. randomly paired individuals.
    d. identical twins.

9. The most common genetically transmitted form of retardation is
    a. psychosis.
    b. schizophrenia.
    c. PKU syndrome.
    d. Down's syndrome.

10. The placenta is the part of the embryo that
    a. attaches to the uterine wall.
    b. eventually becomes the nervous system.
    c. is responsible for temperature regulation.
    d. wards off disease.

11. A fairly specific and stereotyped movement that occurs in response to a specific event (stimulus) is probably a
    a. sensation.
    b. reflex.
    c. conditioned stimulus.
    d. correlated response.

12. Life begins when a single sperm cell unites with the ovum in the female's
    a. placenta.
    b. uterus.
    c. fallopian tube.
    d. vagina.

13. The time between conception and two weeks is called the
    a. germinal period.
    b. embryonic period.
    c. fallopian period.
    d. placenta period.

14. The part of the embryo attached to the uterine wall becomes the
    a. fetus.
    b. embryo.
    c. umbilical cord.
    d. placenta.

15. The part of the body responsible for transporting waste substances from the embryo to the placental barrier is the
    a. placenta.
    b. umbilical cord.
    c. fallopian tube.
    d. uterus

6. The period that lasts from about eight weeks until birth is the
    a. fetal period.
    b. germinal period.
    c. embryonic period.
    d. birthing period.

17. The disease contracted by the mother during the first three months of pregnancy that can cause mental retardation in the infant is
    a. venereal disease.
    b. chicken pox.
    c. mumps.
    d. German measles.

18. There are two periods of greatest general growth, infancy and
    a. preschool.
    b. middle childhood.
    c. adolescence.
    d. adulthood.

19. The part of the brain just above the medulla oblongata and consisting of a number of fibers connecting the two hemi-spheres of the cerebellum and a separate set of fibers connecting the medulla with the cerebrum is called the
    a. midbrain.
    b. pons.
    c. telencephalon.
    d. interbrain.

20. Development of the brain and central nervous system begins shortly after
    a. conception.
    b. two weeks.
    c. one month.
    d. two months.

Comprehension

1. You are a child psychologist who is interested in determining whether mental illness is genetically determined. Discuss two strategies presented in the text that you can use to research this important question.

2. You are a child development specialist and have been asked by your local PTA to make a presentation on environmental influences on prenatal development. Indicate what information you will include in your lecture.

Application

Pay a visit to the maternity ward at your local hospital. Find the part of the ward where all the newborn infants are located. Carefully observe a newborn infant that is a few hours old. Make detailed notes regarding the infant's appearance and movements.

Then observe a two-day-old infant and make the same detailed observations.

1. Describe in detail the newborn infant's appearance.

2. Describe in detail the newborn infant's movements.

3. Describe in detail the two-day-old infant's appearance.

4. Describe in detail the two-day-old infant's movements.

5. Compare the appearance and movements of the two infants. What specific differences were most obvious to you?

Answers

Self-Review

1. b	6. c	11. b	16. a
2. d	7. b	12. c	17. d
3. c	8. a	13. a	18. c
4. a	9. d	14. d	19. b
5. b	10. a	15. b	20. a

1. Twin studies, consanguinity studies
2. Drugs, alcohol, the mother's physical health and emotional state

---

3 Infant Development and Early Experience

Objectives

When you have mastered the material in this chapter, you will be able to—

1. discuss the birth process;
2. list and discuss the capabilities of the newborn infant;
3. describe the infant's sensory capabilities at birth and how these change;
4. describe the developmental changes in children's attention processes;
5. discuss the infant's perception of space;
6. describe the infant's preference for patterns;
7. describe developmental changes in perception of the human face;
8. describe the three aspects of critical periods;
9. describe the importance for rich stimulation for infants.

Key Terms

accommodation
attachment
Babinski reflex
binocular cues
Caesarian birth
cephalo-caudal pattern
convergence
divergence
high-risk infants
innate
Leboyer method
monocular cues
Moro reflex

neonate
object permanence
optimal mismatch
perception
proximo-distal development
retinal disparity
rooting reflex
sensation
short-term birth
size constancy
vergence
visual acuity
visual cliff

Synopsis

I. Introduction
  A. The philosophical debate over the _____   innate
     versus acquired aspects of development has contributed
     to an explosion of knowledge about infancy.
  B. Advances in research _____ have   techniques
     made complex infant abilities measurable.
  C. Most classic theories of development emphasize the
     importance of events that occur during
     _____ . Examples are the oral and anal   infancy
     conflicts theorized by _____ and   Freud's
     Piaget's _____ stage.   sensorimotor
  D. A final stimulus for the interest in infancy is the
     diagnosis and prevention of _____   birth
     _____ .   defects

II. Birth and the Newborn
  A. A few days or weeks before the child is born, the fetus
     becomes positioned head _____ , with   downward
     legs and feet extended _____ .   upward
     1. The next step is labor, the activity by which the
        infant is pushed out of the mother's womb. Labor is
        signaled by the onset of contractions in the uterus.
        A contraction is an involuntary _____   narrowing
        and _____ of the uterine cavity.   lengthening
     2. Eventually the contractions and the baby's head
        pushing down widen the _____   cervix
        enough for the head to pass through. Next the head
        must pass through the _____ ,   pelvis
        a curving, bony passageway, and finally through
        the _____ , the opening of the   perineum
        pelvis.
     3. The physician may need to guide the infant
        through the birth canal with _____ .   forceps
     4. If the fetus is improperly positioned or the birth
        canal is too small a _____   Caesarian
        _____ takes place.   birth
  B. A French physician, _____ , proposed   Leboyer
     a postdelivery environment that minimizes the
     _____ _____   birth shock
     for the infant.
     1. Extraneous _____ is kept to a   noise
        minimum and the room is dimly lit.

2. Immediately after birth the newborn is placed on the mother's _____ .   abdomen

3. The infant is not _____ to start the breathing process.   spanked

C. Not all babies are born on schedule; some are born _____ than expected. A full-term infant is one who has grown in the womb for the full thirty-seven to forty weeks from conception to delivery.   earlier

  1. Generally speaking, a baby weighing four pounds or less is considered _____ _____ or, if born at full term, a _____ _____ .   short-term / birth / high risk

  2. Premature infants often have difficulty _____ , sleeping regularly, and warding off simple germs and infections so they are placed in the protective environment of an _____ .   breathing / incubator

D. Full-term and prematurely born children differ somewhat in infancy.

  1. For about six months after birth premature infants _____ less regularly, _____ more while awake, exhibit less interest in novel events, and develop social responses more _____ than full-term infants.   sleep / cry / slowly

  2. Differences in intelligence and school achievement between children born full-term and short-term are usually attributable to the very smallest of the prematurely born children who may have suffered some _____ or _____ impairment.   neural / physical

E. The head of the newborn infant is _____ in comparison to the rest of the body. A light coating (vernix) appears on the skin.   huge

F. The neonate is now seen as an active individual who picks up information through primitive, but nonetheless workable, _____ apparatus—eyes, ears, nose, mouth, and skin.   perceptual

G. Each of the basic senses is operating at birth, with the possible exception of _____ , about which there is some disagreement.   taste

H. The neonate interacts with the environment by means of several _____ responses. A _____ is a fairly specific and stereotyped movement that occurs in response to a specific event (stimulus).

reflex

reflex

    1. In the _____ reflex the infant curls the toes upward if a fine object is moved quickly across the sole of the foot from the toes toward the heel.

Babinski

    2. In the _____ reflex the infant's back stiffens and the arms extend when he or she is supported in only one place.

Moro

    3. In the _____ reflex, when stroked near the corner of the mouth, the infant opens the mouth and turns the head in the direction of the stimulation.

rooting

    4. The neonate's reflexive _____ in response to a bright light or a loud noise is _____ .

blink

adaptive

III. Motor Behavior and Growth

  A. Although at birth the newborn is physically limited to reflex actions, within a few months dramatic changes occur in the infant's physical capabilities.

    1. Many reflexes have diminished by _____ or _____ months.

four

five

    2. The ability to lift the _____ and _____ develops in the first few months.

head

chest

  B. Control of the head

    1. Growth follows a _____ pattern.

cephalo-caudal

    2. At birth, babies are able to move their heads a little from side to side—most easily when they are lying on their _____ .

backs

    3. By five months, an infant is able to hold his or her head erect while in a _____ position.

sitting

  C. Control of trunk and arms

    1. The infant has little coordination of the chest and arms _____ _____ .

at

birth

2. The ability to hold the _____ up   chest
   while in a face-down position and the ability to
   reach for objects placed in the infant's line of vision
   develop by three to four months.
3. By five months, the infant can _____   sit
   _____ with some support and   up
   grasp objects.
4. By six months, the infant can _____   roll
   _____ when lying in a prone   over
   position.

D. Use and support of legs
   1. The neonate's legs are capable of supporting
      _____ weight.   some
   2. It is not until _____ or   eight
      _____ months that the infant can   nine
      walk with limited help from an adult.
   3. Although the age at which an infant walks for the
      first time varies, the _____ of   sequence
      accomplishments remains fairly uniform.

E. Fine control and coordination
   1. Infant growth is both cephalo-caudal and
      _____ .   proximo-distal
   2. Maturation of the trunk and arms precedes that of
      the _____ and   hands
      _____ .   fingers
   3. The _____ areas of the cortex   association
      bring the areas of the brain that direct movement
      in touch with areas of the brain that detect objects.
   4. The infant does not systematically grasp and hold
      objects until _____ or   four
      _____ months.   five
   5. Stacking and writing activities can be used to
      determine the degree to which the _____   eyes
      and _____ are working together.   hands

IV. Early Sensory Capabilities
    A. Hearing
       1. Fetal monitoring reveals that the fetus can hear
          sounds while in the _____ .   uterus
       2. Newborns prefer _____   high
          _____ sounds and develop early   frequency
          preferences for one voice over others.

3. Newborns distinguish various consonant sounds that differ from one another in only small degrees. Moreover, they distinguish the sounds in much the same way that _____ do, using certain _____ features as cues for the category to which each sound belongs.

       adults
       auditory

B. Touch
  1. Newborns are sensitive to touch, as evidenced by the reflexes mentioned (e.g., Babinski, Moro, rooting), which occur in response to _____ stimulation.

       tactile

  2. Contemporary theories of infant _____ have stressed the importance of tactile sensations for promoting social growth.

       attachment

C. Taste
  1. The sense of taste is one of the more difficult to study because it is intimately involved with the sense of _____ .

       smell

  2. The newborn is sensitive to _____ tastes and can distinguish salt, sugar, lemon juice, and quinine. Newborns enjoy the taste of _____ .

       strong

       sugar

D. Smell
  1. Newborns are sensitive to very strong odors, such as those produced by ammonia and onion.
  2. Newborns seem to adapt to odors that are presented _____ .

       repeatedly

  3. Infants learn the unique odor of their mothers' breasts by six to ten _____ .

       days

E. Vision
  1. Although _____ _____ at birth is poor, young infants do respond to light-dark contrast and variations of movement, color, and brightness.

       visual
       activity

  2. It can be inferred that an infant has _____ between two objects when the infant looks longer at one object that differs from another in some important aspect.

       discriminated

  3. Color _____ in infants may be related to other characteristics associated with color rather than the color itself.

       preferences

4. The infant's eyes are not well _____   coordinated
   at birth. In children and adults, the two eyes work
   together to _____ on objects and   focus
   to perceive depth; in the newborn each eye
   functions as a semi-independent
   _____ of information. Hence, the   receptor
   neonate's perception of the world is very distorted.

5. Normally, in focusing on objects the two eyes may
   converge or diverge. _____ is the   Convergence
   turning inward of the eyes to view an object close
   at hand. _____ is the turning   Divergence
   outward of the eyes to view an object far away.

6. To focus on an object, the _____   lens
   of each eye must also make adjustments for the
   distance between the eye and the object. These
   adjustments of the _____ are   lens
   referred to as accommodation.

7. The newborn's eyes do not _____ ;   accommodate
   each eye seems to have a fixed lens adjustment, set
   for objects about eight to twelve inches away. By
   three or four months of age, however, the infant's
   focusing power is virtually as flexible as that of an
   adult.

V. Visual Perception
   A. Attention
      1. The newborn is interested in _____   geometric
         patterns such as circles and triangles and selects a
         small portion of the _____ figure   geometric
         for examination rather than scanning to inspect the
         whole figure.
      2. When shown a representation of the human face,
         older infants spend more time examining the
         _____ detail of the face, while   internal
         younger infants concentrate on areas on the
         _____ contour of the face.   outer
   B. Space perception
      1. To effectively navigate in our environment, we rely
         on a number of useful perceptions, such as the
         perception of distance and the relative position of
         objects in space. Sources of information for
         perception of distance and depth are

_____ (based on the interaction of   binocular
the two eyes) and _____ (based   monocular
on the use of only one eye).

2. Two binocular cues are _____   vergence
   and _____   retinal

   _____ .   disparity

   a) With _____ , when the eyes   vergence
     converge or diverge in focusing on an object,
     this muscular action can be interpreted by the
     brain to indicate how far away the object is.
     The greater the _____ , the   divergence
     greater the distance.

   b) With _____   retinal

     _____ , each eye has a slightly   disparity
     different view of an object. The greater the
     degree of difference (disparity) between the
     views, the

     _____ the object.   closer

3. _____ cues include   Monocular
   accommodation, perspective, and coloring and
   shading in the visual field.

4. Depth perception can be measured by Walk's and
   Gibson's _____   visual

   _____ .   cliff

5. A major aspect of space perception is the
   perception of size and the _____   size

   _____ of objects.   constancy

6. Based on knowledge about how far away an object
   is and the apparent (retinal) size of the object, the
   observer automatically makes a

   _____ inference about the actual   perceptual
   size of the object.

7. _____ _____ is   Size constancy
   the perceptual recognition that an object is the
   same size in the face of different apparent (retinal)
   sizes.

8. From the age of five or six years a child's ability to
   judge _____ _____   size constancy
   undergoes very little change.

C. Pattern and form
    1. Young infants prefer _____ to   curved
       straight-line figures, drawings with more and larger
       elements, and patterns with _____   larger
       elements rather than _____   more
       elements.
    2. Infants seem to prefer forms that are both
       _____ and moderately discrepant   meaningful
       from the familiar.
    3. Eleanor Gibson concluded that the infant masters a
       sequence of steps in progressing toward full
       _____ appreciation of the face.   perceptual

VI. The Importance of Early Experiences
  A. Critical periods
    1. In Erikson's theory, infancy is a critical period for
       acquiring _____ ; while in Piaget's   trust
       theory, infancy is the time for acquiring
       _____ thought.   sensorimotor
    2. There are three aspects of a critical period.
      a) A particular accomplishment is most likely to
         occur in one period of the _____   life-span
         rather than others.
      b) If the quality does not develop during the
         specific _____ , it is unlikely   period
         to develop thereafter.
      c) The development or nondevelopment of the
         quality in the specified period should have
         consequences for later _____ .   acquisitions
    3. In terms of likelihood of occurrence, infancy is a
       critical period for three well-known phenomena.
      a) When the child will search for a hidden object,
         the child has acquired the concept of
         _____ _____ . object permanence
      b) When the child begins producing two-word
         sentences, the child is using
         _____ .   language
      c) When the child seeks proximity to specific
         caregivers only, the child is evidencing
         _____ .   attachment

B. Both theory and research support the need for rich
stimulation in infancy.
1. Psychoanalytic theory emphasizes the need for
_____ and   predictability
_____ in infant stimulation. comfort
2. Cognitive developmental theory emphasizes the
need for the events in the infant's environment to
strike an _____   optimal
_____ between the infant's current mismatch
level of cognitive function and the next level.
   a) To help a child achieve visually guided
      reaching, display objects and then immediately
      place the object in the infant's

      _____ .   hands
   b) Infants will explore _____ moderately
      _____ events such as a picture novel
      of a face that is slightly dissimilar from the
      expected.
3. In the ethological view, an infant must be
stimulated in ways destined to trigger biologically
_____ responses such as smiling. built-in
Mutual infant/caregiver smiling reflects their
pleasure, but also _____ them binds
together.

Exercises

Self-Review

Circle the letter of the best response.

1. Most theories of development emphasize the importance of
   events that occur during infancy. Examples are the oral and
   anal conflicts theorized by
   a. Piaget.
   b. Freud.
   c. Harlow.
   d. Leboyer.

2. An important stimulus for the interest in infancy research is
   the prevention of
   a. PKU syndrome.
   b. premature deliveries.
   c. sudden infant death syndrome.
   d. birth defects.

3. If the fetus is improperly positioned or the birth canal is too small the doctor must perform
   a. a premature delivery.
   b. an operation.
   c. a caesarian section.
   d. amniocentesis.

4. The French physician who proposed a birth environment that minimizes birth shock and noise is
   a. Leboyer.
   b. Piaget.
   c. Binet.
   d. Monet.

5. The name given to the reflex in which the infant's back stiffens and the arm extends when he or she is supported in only one place is the
   a. Babinski reflex.
   b. Moro reflex.
   c. rooting reflex.
   d. adaptive reflex.

6. Many reflexes lose their strength by
   a. twelve or thirteen months.
   b. ten or eleven months.
   c. seven or eight months.
   d. four or five months.

7. Currently, researchers attribute differences between full-term and short-term infants to
   a. psychological or genetic impairments.
   b. neural or physical impairments.
   c. hormonal or growth impairments.
   d. reflexive or adaptive impairments.

8. The pattern that growth follows is
   a. cephalo-caudal.
   b. proximo-distal.
   c. standardized.
   d. developmental.

9. An infant can sit up with some support at
   a. three months.
   b. four months.
   c. five months.
   d. six months.

10. Maturation of the trunk and arms precedes that of the
    a. shoulders and chest.
    b. hands and fingers.
    c. legs and feet.
    d. eyes and hands.

11. Activities used to determine how the eyes and hands are working together are
    a. stacking and writing.
    b. drawing and stacking.
    c. writing and drawing.
    d. writing and gazing.

12. Olfaction is another name for the sense of
    a. hearing.
    b. taste.
    c. smell.
    d. sight.

13. Convergence is the turning inward of the eyes to view an object
    a. closer to the viewer.
    b. farther from the viewer.
    c. at intermediate distances.
    d. at telescopic distances.

14. Adjustment of the lens of the eye in focusing on objects is known as
    a. convergence.
    b. accommodation.
    c. assimilation.
    d. divergence.

15. A full-term infant has grown in the womb for
    a. twenty-nine to thirty-two weeks.
    b. thirty-one to thirty-four weeks.
    c. thirty-four to thirty-seven weeks.
    d. thirty-seven to forty weeks.

16. Visual cues to distance with only one eye involved are called
    a. perspectives.
    b. retinal disparities.
    c. monocular cues.
    d. binocular cues.

17. The visual cliff measures
    a. illusions.
    b. depth perception.
    c. distinctive features.
    d. similarity.

18. According to Erikson, infancy is a critical period for the development of
    a. trust.
    b. attachment.
    c. object permanence.
    d. language.

19. When a child will search for a hidden object, the child has acquired the concept of
    a. familiar figures.
    b. transductive reasoning.
    c. retinal disparity.
    d. object permanence.

20. Attachment is said to occur when the child seeks
    a. attention.
    b. affection.
    c. proximity.
    d. nurturance.

Comprehension

1. You are a developmental psychologist who is interested in infant preferences for various kinds of stimulus information. Construct a study that can be used to determine whether infants prefer looking at one-color stimuli or multi-colored stimuli. For your study incorporate the techniques developed by Robert Fantz.

2. Develop a study to determine age changes in infant's perception of depth.

Application

1. Locate an infant in your neighborhood or at a day-care center. Construct six different patterns on different pieces of paper, varying the color and the amount of detail in each. Show the infant the patterns one at a time, each for one minute, and record the number of seconds that the infant looks at each pattern. In the space below describe the patterns that the infant looked at longest. Were certain colors associated with those patterns? Were more complex patterns looked at longer than simple patterns?

2. In an experiment exploring the infant's ability to pinpoint the direction of sound, T. G. R. Bower found that infants less than six months old are fairly accurate in locating objects directly ahead of them but poor in locating objects to their right or left. With an infant less than six months old, test Bower's conclusions. Make a pleasant noise directly ahead of the infant, 30 degrees to the infant's right, and 30 degrees to the infant's left. Record whether or not the infant appears to reach toward the noise. Were your results similar to Bower's? If not, discuss how they were different.

Answers

Self-Review

1. b	6. d	11. a	16. c
2. d	7. b	12. c	17. b
3. c	8. a	13. a	18. a
4. a	9. c	14. b	19. d
5. b	10. b	15. d	20. c

Comprehension

1. Present a pair of stimuli (drawings) to an infant. One stimulus in each pair should contain only one color; the second should contain several different colors. Observe which of the two stimuli in each pair the infant looks at longer.

2. Use the visual cliff apparatus developed by Walk and Gibson for measuring depth perception. Select infants of different ages, and place them on the visual cliff apparatus. Observe and record whether the infants back away from the cliff or proceed to cross it with little or no hesitation.

---

4 Learning and Development

Objectives

When you have mastered the material in this chapter, you will be able to—

1. define learning and describe it;
2. describe five kinds of learning—classical conditioning, operant conditioning, imitation, concept learning, and rule learning;
3. identify and define basic features of learning—generalization, discrimination, shaping, and extinction;
4. describe the basic conditions of learning;
5. discuss Gibson's theory of perceptual learning.

Key Terms

abstractness
behavior modification
classical conditioning
closure
competence motivation
concept
concept learning
conditioned response
conditioned stimulus
discrimination
distinctive feature

extinction
figure and ground
generalization
Gestalt
good continuation
holistic
hypotheses
imitation
interval schedule
learning
learning sets

mediators	reinforcement
motivation	rule
negative reinforcement	rule learning
observational learning	schedules of reinforcement
operant conditioning	secondary reinforcers
partial schedule	sets
perceptual learning	shaping
primary reinforcers	similarity
proximity	unconditioned response
punishment	unconditioned stimulus
ratio schedule	variable schedule

Synopsis

I. Definition of Learning

    A. When the term learning is used by psychologists, it refers to a change in behavior that occurs as a result of _____ .   experience

    B. Some responses are not the result of learning. _____ are responses that are wired into a person's nervous system. They occur without any practice.   Reflexes

    C. There are also responses that are influenced by experience but depend on physical maturation and growth processes. Such responses are _____ rather than learned.   maturational

II. Kinds of Learning

    A. _____ _____ was first described by the Russian psychologist Ivan Pavlov.   Classical conditioning

        1. In classical conditioning it is assumed that learning occurs through a simple _____ _____ association. A stimulus is any event in the environment that initially causes some response to be made by the organism. For example, the presentation of food powder to a hungry dog causes the dog to salivate. The food powder is an _____ ; the act of salivation is an _____ _____ .   stimulus-response

unconditioned stimulus unconditioned response

        2. When another stimulus, a buzzer, is presented at the same time as the food, it does not cause the dog to salivate; it is a _____ stimulus.   neutral

However, when the buzzer is repeatedly presented with the food, the dog eventually salivates when the buzzer is presented alone. The buzzer is referred to as a _____ _____ .   conditioned stimulus

When the dog salivates to the sound of the buzzer alone, the salivation is a _____   conditioned

_____ .   response

3. John B. Watson popularized the concept of classical conditioning in the United States by writing extensively about its occurrence in everyday situations. His most famous experimental work today is his demonstration of conditioning in a one-year-old child named _____ .   Albert

4. Clinical psychologists today believe that the many fears adults harbor but cannot explain are due to early _____ .   conditioning

B. _____ _____ is a   Operant conditioning form of learning most recently described by B. F. Skinner.

1. In classical conditioning the initial unconditioned response is _____ , or spontaneous,   reflexive to a specific stimulus at the onset of conditioning. In operant conditioning the response initially occurs freely, not in reaction to a specific

_____ .   stimulus

2. A response that is followed by a pleasant consequence is more likely to recur; this effect on the response is called _____ . A   reinforcement response followed by an unpleasant experience is less likely to recur; this effect is called

_____ .   punishment

3. According to Skinner, if an event follows a response and the response is repeated, the event is a _____ whether it is pleasant or   reinforcer unpleasant.

4. In _____ _____ it   negative reinforcement is the removal of a stimulus that causes a response to recur.

5. The consequences to a child for emitting a certain behavior may be governed by different schedules of reinforcement or punishment. A _____ is the rule that explains   schedule when the consequence occurs in relation to the behavior.

a) In an _____ schedule,   interval
consequences are specified by time.

b) In a _____ schedule,   ratio
consequences are specified by the frequency of
the specific behaviors.

c) In _____ schedules the   variable
interval or ratio contingency changes value
from one occasion to the next.

d) In _____ schedules one is   partial
sometimes rewarded and sometimes not for a
particular response.

6. Operant conditioning has had practical implications
in self-paced learning and programmed instruction
as well as in _____ modification.   behavior

C. Another type of learning involves simple observation
and _____ .   imitation

1. Several years ago Neal Miller and John Dollard
proposed an influential theory of
_____ (imitative) learning. They   observational
stated that people imitate what others do because
the imitative responses are

_____ .   reinforced

2. Albert Bandura has proposed that observational
learning can occur in the absence of
_____ . According to Bandura, it is   reinforcement
important to distinguish between acquistion of
responses through observation and
_____ of them once they have   performance
have been learned.

D. In _____ learning the same response is   concept
learned for an entire class of situations or events.

1. There are a number of different views about how
concepts are learned. One is that the learner
acquires _____ , or a tendency to   sets
notice that certain responses inherently belong with
certain kinds of events.

2. A second view is that children develop
_____ , mental steps that intervene   mediators
between the presentation of a stimulus and the
response made to it. The mediator is viewed as an
internalized _____   stimulus-
_____ association that guides   response
behavior directed toward external events.

3. Yet another view is that children approach a task with a number of _____ about what properties are part of the stimulus class in question.   hypotheses

E. _____ learning is one of the highest possible forms of learning, according to Gagne.   Rule

   1. A rule is a relation between two or more _____ . Rule learning depends on the child's having previously mastered the concepts that make up the _____ .   concepts / rule

   2. The _____ and _____ of concepts contained in the rule also influence the difficulty of learning it.   number / abstractness

F. Perceptual learning focuses upon changes in the way _____ are interpreted and represented.   stimuli

   1. The _____ view is that perception is organized and dictated by several properties of the perceptual field.   Gestalt

     a) A major property of the perceptual field is that perception of it is a _____ event; the whole is something different from the sum of its parts—hence the term _____ .   holistic / Gestalt

     b) The forces that determine how the field is perceived are called the laws of _____ and include the principles of similarity, _____ , closure, and good continuation.   organization / proximity

   2. Eleanor Gibson views perceptual change as a _____ process.   gradual

     a) The child becomes aware of features of the environment that have gone _____ before.   unnoticed

     b) The child takes an _____ part in perception.   active

     c) Perception is _____ by nature.   selective

III. Basic Features of Learning

A. _____ depends upon the similarity between new and old stimuli.   Generalization

1. Generalization is a feature of learning in which a _____ occurs in the presence of an event that is similar, but not identical, to the one present when it was first learned.

       response

2. The degree to which generalization occurs depends upon the similarity between new and old _____ .

       stimuli

B. _____ is the inverse of generalization. The ability to discriminate is revealed by the extent to which a child does not respond to an event that is _____ from the one to which the response was originally learned.

       Discrimination

       different

C. _____ is the gradual approximation of a desired response through reinforcement. Skinner first showed that zero-level entry behavior can be shaped gradually through successive _____ to produce the final, desired response.

       Shaping

       proximations

D. _____ is used to see how well a particular behavior has been learned and to demonstrate that most learned behaviors can also be _____ .

       Extinction

       unlearned

1. In classical conditioning _____ refers to the phase after a conditioned response has been established.

       extinction

2. In operant conditioning extinction refers to the phase in which the reinforcer is _____ . A response that continues without reinforcement will eventually _____ .

       discontinued

       disappear

E. Primary and secondary reinforcers can be distinguished.

1. If an infant's vocalizing is increased by tactile stimulation, the tactile stimulation is a _____ reinforcer.

       primary

2. Later the infant may vocalize in the mere presence of the person who provided stimulation. The sight of the person is a _____ reinforcer.

       secondary

F. Reinforcement history is unique for each child; an event that is _____ for one may not be for another.

       reinforcing

G. Competence _____ enhances learning.

       motivation

1. The degree to which children need _____ rewards to enhance learning may vary.

       external

2. Robert White presented a compelling argument for the idea that people often _____ learn for the sheer joy of mastering a behavior.

Exercises

Self-Review

Circle the letter of the best response.

1. Pavlov is best known for his research and writing regarding
   a. operant conditioning.
   b. classical conditioning.
   c. observational learning.
   d. extinction.

2. Skinner is best known for his research and writing regarding
   a. operant conditioning.
   b. classical conditioning.
   c. observational learning.
   d. extinction.

3. A conditioned stimulus is a
   a. response that occasions behavior.
   b. response that always elicited a stimulus.
   c. formerly neutral stimulus that elicits a response.
   d. response that suppresses behavior.

4. A reinforced response
   a. diminishes.
   b. will occur in the future.
   c. will not occur in the future.
   d. gradually fades.

5. A relation between two concepts is known as a
   a. cue.
   b. response.
   c. stimulus.
   d. rule.

6. A response has shown generalization when it
   a. occurs in the presence of a similar stimulus.
   b. occurs in the presence of a dissimilar stimulus.
   c. diminishes.
   d. increases its frequency.

7. Discrimination is
   a. similar to habituation.
   b. similar to observational learning.
   c. the opposite of generalization.
   d. similar to generalization.

8. Which one of the following terms is *not* a Gestalt principle of perception?
   a. similarity
   b. proximity
   c. closure
   d. differentiation

9. When Johnnie's teacher praises him for his classwork, she is using
   a. classical conditioning.
   b. tutoring.
   c. reinforcement.
   d. punishment.

10. When Tony's alarm clock rings every morning he quickly turns it off to stop the ringing. He learned to turn his alarm clock off through the use of
    a. positive reinforcement.
    b. negative reinforcement.
    c. punishment.
    d. shaping.

11. When a mother yells at her son for the same behavior day after day she is
    a. reinforcing the behavior.
    b. punishing the behavior.
    c. shaping the behavior.
    d. extinguishing the behavior.

12. A friend of Bonnie's teased her when she wore an orange dress. She is so embarrassed she never wears orange dresses. This is an example of
    a. shaping.
    b. modeling.
    c. reinforcement.
    d. punishment.

13. Money is a
    a. unconditioned stimulus.
    b. conditioned stimulus.
    c. primary reinforcer.
    d. secondary reinforcer.

14. Gibson argues that perceptual change is
    a. immediate.
    b. gradual.
    c. all or none.
    d. incomplete.

15. According to Bandura, the element *not* necessary for learning to occur is
    a. attention.
    b. memory.
    c. reinforcement.
    d. *a* and *b*.

16. An emphasis on consequences is usually associated with
    a. observational learning.
    b. operant conditioning.
    c. classical conditioning.
    d. imitation.

17. Within which of the following theoretical orientations does classical conditioning fit?
    a. psychoanalytic
    b. cognitive-structural
    c. S-R
    d. humanistic

18. When a response is reinforced occasionally, we say it is being
    a. shaped.
    b. punished.
    c. continuously reinforced.
    d. intermittently reinforced.

19. Food and warmth are
    a. primary reinforcers.
    b. secondary reinforcers.
    c. punishers.
    d. shapers.

20. When the probability of a response decreases following the application of an aversive stimulus, the response has been
    a. reinforced.
    b. punished.
    c. extinguished.
    d. shaped.

Comprehension

The following examples represent different kinds of learning that you read about in chapter 4. Below each example indicate the kind of learning that is illustrated.

1. A young boy was playing with a toy train. While he was playing, a large crash of thunder occurred and scared him. From that day on, the child did not want to play with his toy train because it frightened him.

2. Every time her mother refused to give Jan an extra helping of dessert, Jan cried. Since her mother felt bad at the thought of making Jan cry, she always let Jan have more dessert.

3. Tommy was watching his favorite cartoon program on television. The cartoon characters on this program always used aggressive behaviors to obtain what they desired. One day when Tommy was playing with his friends, he remembered what his favorite cartoon characters did when they wanted to get their way, and he began behaving aggressively with his friends.

4. During the first week of school Joan's first-grade teacher taught the children that all four-legged animals that bark are called dogs.

5. Paul's fifth-grade teacher taught him that combining the colors blue and green results in the color yellow.

Application

1. Psychologists have found that children can be reinforced vicariously; that is, children who watch other children receive reinforcement for a behavior may themselves be reinforced for that behavior. To demonstrate the impact of vicarious reinforcement, arrange two groups of preschool children, four children to a group. Working with only one group at a time, give each child paper and crayons and ask the group to draw a simple picture of the outdoors. While the children are drawing, approach one child in the group and with enthusiasm tell the child how much you like some particular part of his or her picture—the clouds, for example. When the drawings are finished, collect them. With the second group of preschoolers, follow the same procedure but do not provide the vicarious reinforcement. Keeping separate records for each group, count the number of times the vicariously reinforced object (i.e., clouds) appears in the drawings of both groups. In which group of drawings does the vicariously reinforced object appear more often? Did the children in the first group respond to the vicarious reinforcement? Did the child whose picture you commented on with enthusiasm respond to the direct reinforcement?

Answers

Self-Review

1. b		11. a	
2. a		12. d	
3. c		13. d	
4. b		14. b	
5. d		15. c	
6. a		16. b	
7. c		17. c	
8. d		18. d	
9. c		19. a	
10. b		20. b	

Comprehension

1. classical conditioning
2. operant conditioning
3. imitation
4. concept learning
5. rule learning

Part 2 Cognitive Development

---

5 Piaget's Theory of Intellectual Development

Objectives

When you have mastered the material in this chapter, you will be able to—

1. define cognitive development;
2. describe and discuss the processes and stages of cognitive development postulated by Piaget;
3. evaluate Piaget's theory;
4. discuss the neo-Piagetian approaches to cognitive development.

Key Terms

accommodation
animism
assimilation
automaticity
centration
classify
concrete operations stage
conservation
contrary-to-fact reasoning
deductive-hypothesis
egocentrism
equilibration
formal operations stage

irreversibility
Jean Piaget
metaphor
neo-Piagetian
object permanence
preoperations stage
qualitative
relativism
reversibility
schema
sensorimotor stage
serialization
symbol

Synopsis

I. The best known cognitive theorist of the twentieth century was the Swiss psychologist _____ _____ .

          Jean Piaget

II. Piaget's theory of cognitive development postulates that the child passes through a series of stages of thought from infancy to adolescence.

  A. Passage through the stages is the result of biological pressures to adapt to the environment and to organize structures of thinking. These stages of thought are described as qualitatively different from one another in contrast to the quantitative assessments of intellect made in standard intelligence tests.

  B. The stage that lasts from birth to about two years of age (infancy) is the _____ stage. The infant's mental development consists of progress in the ability to organize and coordinate sensations and perceptions with physical movements and actions. This stage is subdivided into six substages that demarcate changes in the nature of sensorimotor organization. Because this is a stage theory, these changes must be _____ .

          sensorimotor

          qualitative

    1. During substage 1 the infant develops the ability to produce behaviors that resemble reflexes in the absence of obvious reflex stimuli.

2. During substage 2 the infant learns to coordinate sensation and action with habits and primary circular reactions. A habit is based upon simple reflexes. A primary circular reaction is based upon the infant's attempt to reproduce an interesting or pleasurable event that initially occurred by chance.

3. During substage 3 the infant becomes more object oriented, or focused on the surrounding world, and moves beyond preoccupation with self in sense-action interactions. Although directed toward objects in the world, the infant's actions lack an intentional, goal-directed quality.

4. During substage 4 the infant readily combines and recombines previously learned actions in a coordinated fashion. Related to this coordination is the second achievement—the presence of intentionality, the separation of means and goals in accomplishing simple feats.

5. In substage 5 the infant purposefully explores new possibilities with objects, continuously changing what is done to them and exploring the results. Piaget speaks of this period as marking the developmental starting point for human curiosity and interest in novelty.

6. During substage 6 the infant's mental functioning shifts from a purely sensorimotor plane to a symbolic plane. (For Piaget, a symbol is an internalized sensory image or word that represents an event.)

C. One of the infant's most significant sensorimotor accomplishments is the ability to understand that objects and events continue to exist even when he or she is not in direct perceptual contact with them. This is called _____ _____ .   object permanence

1. During substage 1 there is no apparent object permanence.

2. During substage 2 there is a primitive form of object permanence.

3. During substage 3 the infant's sense of object permanence undergoes further development. With this newfound ability to coordinate simple actions, the infant shows clear patterns of searching for a missing object.

4. During substage 4 the infant's knowledge or belief in the continued existence of the missing object is stronger than it was in the previous substage.
5. During substage 5 the infant can apparently hold an image or a missing object in mind longer than in substage 4.
6. During substage 6 the infant is able to "image" the missing object and to manipulate the "image" (mentally follow it) from one location to the next.

D. The stage that lasts from about two to seven years of age, cutting across the preschool and early elementary-school years, is called the _____ stage.　preoperational

  1. At this stage the child's thought is not yet governed by full-fledged operations. (Internalized sets of actions that allow the child to do mentally what before was done physically are called

    _____ .)　operations

  2. The most salient feature of preoperational thought is the child's inability to distinguish easily between his or her own perspective and that of someone else. This is called _____ .　egocentrism

  3. Another facet of preoperational thought is the belief that inanimate objects have human qualities and are capable of human action. This is called

    _____ .　animism

  4. Yet another characteristic of preoperational thought is the child's failure to conserve properties of objects in the face of superficial changes in their appearance. The skill lacked is called

    _____ .　conservation

  5. Another important limitation of the child's structure of thought in the preoperational stage is the inability to form and reason with hierarchies. Faced with a random collection of objects that can be grouped on the basis of two or more properties, the child is seldom able to use these properties consistently to sort the objects. Thus, the child is unable to _____ .　classify

  6. An important social consequence of these deficits in the young child's thinking with classes is that he or she fails to understand the various ways people can be cross-classified with regard to social characteristics and the different ways people can be compared with a group that includes them.

7. Another feature of preoperational thought is that the child is incapable of ordering a set of objects from least to greatest along some clearly quantifiable dimension. The skill lacked is called

_____ .   serialization

8. Two organizing forces in preoperational thought are centration and irreversibility. A narrow concentration on one feature of a situation to the exclusion of others is called _____ .   centration
The inability to reverse actions mentally is called

_____ .   irreversibility

E. The stage that lasts from about seven to eleven years of age is called the _____   concrete
_____ stage. The concrete thinker has   operations
none of the limitations of the preoperational thinker and is capable of thought in all the respects that the preoperational thinker is not.
   1. This shift to a more perfect system of thinking is brought about by several gradual changes. One of these is the shift away from egocentrism. The child can now decenter, or operate with two or more aspects of a problem simultaneously. This reveals a shift toward _____ .   relativism
   2. Another change, the child's ability to reverse actions, is called _____ .   reversibility
   3. One limitation of concrete thinking is its reliance on clearly available perceptual and physical supports. The child needs to have objects and events on hand in order to think about them, thus the term _____ .   concrete

F. The stage that comes into play between the ages of eleven and fourteen is called the _____   formal
_____ stage. The adolescent is no   operations
longer limited to actual, concrete experience as an anchor for thought.
   1. The make-believe nature of thought can be seen in the adolescent's ability to propose and work with contrary-to-fact reasoning.
   2. Adolescent ability to work with conjured-up possibilities is easily seen in the way they approach problem solving. They formulate a plan to propose and test a series of hypotheses, each of which

narrows the field of choices. This style of problem solving has often been referred to as

_____ _____ .   deductive-hypothesis testing

3. Another property of formal thinking is the ability of the adolescent to appreciate metaphorical meaning. An implied comparison between two ideas that is conveyed by the abstract meaning contained in the words used to make the comparison is called a _____ .   metaphor

G. In Piaget's view, all mental processes—attention, perception, memory, thought—undergo a similar development. Each has its sensorimotor, preoperational, and concrete operational stages, for example. Each activity is not a separate process, as suggested by the information-processing theorists, but a separate reflection of how the child is thinking.

H. Piaget had little to say about thinking during the adult years. He believed adult thought is explained by the capabilities of the stage of _____   formal
_____ . Other writers have speculated   operations
about additional "stages" that would not be universal but rather dependent on experience.

III. Scholars who have studied Piaget now tend to see their task as extending what Piaget began.

A. Piaget was a brilliant observer of children.

B. Piaget gave us many good ideas about what to look for in development.

C. Piaget served up a forceful argument for adults to learn how to deal with children on their own terms because of his view that differences between child and adult thinking are _____ .   qualitative

D. Piaget offered a host of ideas about how the child changes.

1. We make experiences fit our cognitive framework or _____ . This process is called   schemas
_____ .   assimilation

2. We also adjust our cognitive framework to experience. This process is called

_____ .   accommodation

3. Significant cognitive change only comes when our schemas are clearly shown to be inconsistent with each other on the environment. This process is called _____ .   equilibration

E. Piaget has been most widely criticized for his claim of stages. Successful attainment of one conceptual understanding has not been found to predict successful attainment of what researchers believe should be related concepts.

F. Assimilation, accommodation, and equilibration are difficult to operationally pin down.

G. Many of the cognitive phenomena discovered by Piaget do not behave in the way he claimed.

IV. Some scholars are attemping to construct a new theory that preserves Piaget's better insights and observations. Such approaches are called _____ .   neo-Piagetian

A. One influential neo-Piagetian approach is the model of Pascual-Leone and Case.

1. They believe that many Piagetian tasks require several cognitive strategies to solve them.

2. A second notion is that the child's ability to remember information is the key to applying these strategies. The type of memory needed is

_____ .   short-term

3. It is assumed that with practice and experience many strategies can be applied with little or no mental effort. This is referred to as increased

_____ .   automaticity

B. Other neo-Piagetian approaches exist.

1. Feldman emphasizes individual differences.

2. Flavell is interested in the sequence of change, as was Piaget, but he does not hold to Piaget's strong claims about how sequences are interrelated.

3. Fisher emphasizes skills and a fairly universal sequence of change for each skill. Fisher did not, however, believe these skills to be part of a system of stages.

Exercises

Self-Review

Circle the letter of the best response.

1. Change from one cognitive stage to another is said to be
   a. discontinuous.
   b. continuous.
   c. abrupt.
   d. gradual.

2. Which of the following occurs during the sensorimotor stage?
   a. object permanence
   b. conservation
   c. seriation
   d. hypothesis-testing

3. Children believe that inanimate objects have human qualities in the
   a. sensorimotor stage.
   b. preoperational stage.
   c. concrete operations stage.
   d. formal operations stage.

4. When children attend to only one aspect of a situation or problem it is said that they are exhibiting
   a. conservation.
   b. animism.
   c. centration.
   d. seriation.

5. Children begin to display reversibility during the
   a. sensorimotor stage.
   b. preoperational stage.
   c. concrete stage.
   d. formal stage.

6. Children manifest hypothesis testing during the
   a. sensorimotor stage.
   b. preoperational stage.
   c. concrete stage.
   d. formal stage.

7. When two ideas are conveyed by the abstract meanings contained in the words used to make the comparison, it is termed
   a. a metaphor.
   b. centration.
   c. relativism.
   d. a theory.

8. A Piagetian process is
   a. catharsis.
   b. reinforcement.
   c. punishment.
   d. assimilation.

9. Scholars who have built upon Piaget's theorizing are called
   a. Piagetian.
   b. psychocognitive.
   c. structuralists.
   d. neo-Piagetian.

10. Two neo-Piagetian researchers who emphasize short-term memory are
    a. Miller and Dollard.
    b. Flavell and Wellman.
    c. Pascual-Leon and Case.
    d. Harlow and Harlow.

11. Cognitive developmental stages in adulthood are said to be
    a. dependent on experience.
    b. dependent on maturation.
    c. universal.
    d. reversible.

12. Complex mental strategies are called
    a. images.
    b. operations.
    c. schemes.
    d. signals.

13. When a child changes his or her way of thinking to conform to experience he or she has
    a. remembered.
    b. equilibrated.
    c. assimilated.
    d. accommodated.

14. The ability that occurs when a child can order a set of objects is called
    a. relativism.
    b. animism.
    c. serialization.
    d. conservation.

15. The period of concrete operations lasts from approximately
    a. four to seven.
    b. seven to eleven.
    c. twelve to fifteen.
    d. eighteen to twenty-one.

16. When a child is unable to see another person's point of view he or she is
    a. egocentric.
    b. centrated.
    c. animistic.
    d. selfish.

17. When a child believes that an object no longer exists when it is out of sight, the child has not mastered the concept of
    a. class inclusion.
    b. seriation.
    c. object permanence.
    d. reversibility.

18. Most scholars now doubt the notion of
    a. short-term memory.
    b. formal operations.
    c. conservation.
    d. stages.

19. When a number of strategies can be used with little effort there is increased
    a. automaticity.
    b. sequence.
    c. maturation.
    d. relativism.

20. A twelve-year-old is probably in the
    a. sensorimotor stage.
    b. preoperational stage.
    c. concrete operations stage.
    d. formal operations stage.

Comprehension

1. You are a graduate student enrolled in a seminar on cognitive development and you have been asked by the instructor to present an evaluation of Piaget's theory. Write a critique of Piaget's theory that you would present in the seminar. Be sure to include evidence to support your statements.

2. You are a special consultant to a large school district, and the superintendent of the school district has asked you to present an address to the district's elementary school teachers on changes in children's cognitive abilities between the ages five and seven. Write your address in detail.

Application

Piaget classifies children at different stages of cognitive development according to their ability to perform tasks that measure their concept of conservation. Children who have acquired this concept understand that some features of objects remain invariant, despite changes in other features. Three types of conservation are usually assessed: number, mass, and weight. For the following evaluations, work individually with a five-year-old and a seven-year-old.

1. Assess conservation of number. Arrange ten pennies in two rows of five. Ask the five-year-old whether each row includes the same number of pennies. Then spread the pennies apart in one row so that one row is longer than the other, and ask the child again whether each row includes the same number of pennies. Record the child's responses. Repeat the same procedure with the seven-year-old. Did both children demonstrate conservation of number? If not, how were their responses different?

Answers

Self-Review

1. d		11. a
2. a		12. b
3. b		13. d
4. c		14. c
5. c		15. b
6. d		16. a
7. a		17. c
8. d		18. d
9. d		19. a
10. c		20. d

Comprehension

1. All who label themselves Piagetians recognize that his theory is only a tentative, best approximation description of a very complex matter, the development of human thought. According to Piaget, specific thinking skills appear in specific age periods. For the vast majority of skills, these predictions have been confirmed. A growing number of studies question Piaget's age estimates. Piaget's claim that cognitive development is characterized by stagelike properties is the most difficult issue of all. There is as much disconfirming evidence as confirming evidence for Piaget's claims. It is primarily in the realm of stage invariance that the evidence supports Piaget. Finally, dozens of studies have demonstrated that it is possible to accelerate cognitive development, although change in one skill area does not seem to transfer to other skill areas.
2. Your detailed discussion should include changes in the following cognitive skills: conservation, serialization, egocentrism, hierarchical ordering, and class inclusion.

6 Information Processing

Objectives

When you have mastered the material in this chapter, you will be able to—

1. describe the origins of the tradition of information processing;
2. describe the tools of information processing;
3. describe the stages in information processing;
4. describe the nature of perceptual change in childhood;
5. describe the different kinds of memory that play an important role in development;
6. describe the basic processes employed in remembering;
7. describe how basic memory processes change as the child matures;
8. describe problem solving and metacognition.

Key Terms

attention
backward learning curve
chunks
completeness
dichotic listening
elaboration
empirical inferences
evaluative inferences
extrapolative inferences
goal setting
hardware
hemispheric specialization
inference
information processing
lexical inferences
linguistics
logical inferences
long-term memory
memory

metacognition
overlearning
paired associates
parallel processing
perception
problem solving
recall
recognition
redundancy
rehearsal
saccadic movement
salience
selectivity
sensory register
serial processing
short-term memory
software
spatial and temporal
  interpretations
task analysis

Synopsis

I. Introduction
   A. Mental activity is thought to be synonymous with the processing of information in the approach called

   _____ _____ .   information processing

   B. Steps often involved in processing information include attention, perception, memory, thinking, and problem solving.

II. The Roots of Information-Processing Theory
   A. Over a quarter of a century ago, scientists sought to develop a general model of how someone sends a message over a particular channel of communication to a specific receiver. They developed a model of

   _____ .   communication

   B. A second influence on the information-processing approach was the growth of computer science and the interest in using the computer to model theories of artificial intelligence.
      1. Both the computer and the mind employ

      _____ and   logic
      _____ .   rules

      2. Both have limits imposed on how they are capable of handling information and what types of information can be processed.
         a) The physical machinery of the computer is the

         _____ . This hardware   hardware
         compares to the human's brain and nervous system.

         b) The programming in the computer is the

         _____ . Limits placed by the   software
         software are similar to limits placed on the human by learning and development.
   C. The third development is some recent advances by scholars such as Chomsky and Fillmore in the field of

   _____ .   linguistics

III. The Tools of Information Processing
   A. Technology is central to the field of information processing.
      1. The creative inspiration for imagining how the human mind works and the most versatile tool for

managing and evaluating the complex data
collected about the workings of the mind is the
_____ _____ .   high-speed computer
  2. High-speed photography is a second important
     technology. One aspect of which is eye-movement
     photography. The rapid eye activity involved in
     examining the environment can be divided into the
     movements called _____ .   saccadic
B. Another tool of the information-processing approach is
   the division of tasks into primitive steps for
   examination. This is called _____   task
   _____ .   analysis
C. Implicit in most theories of information processing is
   the idea that it takes some measurable amount of time
   to complete each cognitive step in the course of solving
   a task.
  1. As the number of discrete items to process
     increases, the longer is the interval needed to
     process them.
  2. As the number of processing steps increases, the
     longer is the interval needed to execute them.
  3. When additional processing steps are added they
     may be processed in one of two ways. When a
     single mode of processing is used it is called
     _____ . When more than one mode   serial
     is used at a time in processing, the processing is
     called _____ .   parallel
  4. The more automatic a skill is the more likely the
     skill has been _____ .   overlearned

IV. Steps in Information Processing
A. Noticing an event (stimulus) in the environment
   defines _____ .   attention
  1. There seem to be great changes in a young child's
     ability to pay attention during the early childhood
     years.
  2. These changes in attention have a dramatic
     influence on the child's learning.
  3. Young children take much longer than older
     children to attend to features of events that hold
     the key to important actions. This phenomenon has
     been demonstrated by use of the backward learning
     curve.

4. Another feature of attention is the tendency to focus on what is important or relevant to completing the task at hand and weeding out extraneous information. This is called _____ . Vlietstra, Wright, and their colleagues have proposed that the distinction of exploring versus searching new environments constitutes an important shift in IP in children during the school years.

selectivity

5. It is often necessary to sequentially attend to everything in some circumscribed arena; that is, to search in some organized fashion, exhausting all possibilities. This is called _____ .

completeness

6. The ability to screen out other conversations while focusing on what someone is saying is called

_____ _____ .

dichotic listening

   a) Studies in this area indicate that younger children are less able to focus on relevant information.
   b) Another common finding is that children find it easier to track a message coming over the right ear than the left. This is due to

_____ _____ .

hemispheric specialization

B. The interpretation of what is sensed is

_____ .

perception

1. Often young children need to have a lot of information presented under optimal sensory conditions to correctly identify an event. Having more than is necessary or duplicate information is the definition of _____ .

redundancy

2. Another way perception changes in children is in how properties or dimensions of events are noticed. There are at least two types of changes.
   a) One type involves the selection of the dimensions to notice, or the _____ of dimensions.

salience

   b) A second type of change is closely associated with the idea that younger children have undifferentiated perceptions of objects, whereas the perceptions of older children are more differentiated.

3. Yet a third way perception changes is the meaning people attach to what they experience and the ways in which they organize that experience. Researchers have studied the importance of culture in how we perceive drawings of familiar events.

C. The retention of information over time is

_____ .   memory

   1. There are many kinds of memory, each of which may be somewhat independent of the others.

     a) The type of memory involved in remembering a telephone number is _____ .   recall

     b) The type of memory in which you simply indicate which of several events was experienced is _____ .   recognition

     c) The type of memory involved in remembering a person's name when you see the person is

_____ _____ .   paired associates

   2. One prominent view conceives of memory as the flow of information through the human mind.

     a) Memories that last for no more than one second are processed in the

_____ _____ .   sensory register

     b) The memory used to retain ideas and thoughts as you work on problems is

_____ memory.   short-term

   3. Among the processes assumed to be responsible for shifting information to long-term storage are rehearsal, elaboration, organization, and various constructive memory processes.

     a) If a response to a stimulus is repeated it is more likely to be remembered. This repetition is one form of _____ .   rehearsal

     b) You may associate an experience with something familiar to you, generate an image for it, or develop a sentence or short story about it in your mind. This memory process is called

_____ .   elaboration

     c) Unwieldy information may be retained by organizing it into smaller units, or

_____ .   chunks

     d) A more common way to organize information is to place items into meaningful

_____ .   categories

D. A relation noted between one event and another that is
not directly stated is an _____ .   inference
   1. There are different types of inferences.
      a) If we need not even experience the events
         directly to understand how they are related to
         one another, the connection between events is

         _____ .   logical
      b) If we need to have some specialized experiences
         with the type of circumstances being described
         to arrive at the correct inference, the
         connection between events is

         _____ .   empirical
      c) Another distinction among types of inferences
         is that of literal vs. nonliteral.
   2. There is abundant evidence to show that children
      improve dramatically in their abilities to draw
      certain types of inferences as they mature.
   3. But the more interesting matter is the nature of the
      processes that underly successful inferential
      activity.
      a) An important part of drawing inferences is
         knowing when to do so.
      b) The importance of what the individual already
         knows influences what he or she will get out of
         some cognitive encounter. This prior knowledge
         is called _____ and   scripts
         _____ _____ .   semantic networks
      c) Children may have equivalent knowledge bases,
         but they have different abilities to quickly
         retrieve the information at the moment it is
         needed.
   4. Scholars have suggested additional classes of
      inferences.
      a) Interpretations of words that may have more
         than one meaning in a text are

         _____ _____ .   lexical inferences
      b) Interpretations given to story events that
         situate them in appropriate place and time are
         _____ and   spatial
         _____ _____ .   temporal interpretations
      c) Guesses about what happened in the past and
         surmises about what might happen next are
         involved in _____   extrapolative
         _____ .   inferences

d) Gauging the significance of an event, deciding whether it is a normal or surprising occurrence, and establishing its moral value are involved in _____ _____ .

    evaluative inferences

E. Processing information to fulfill a major goal is the definition of _____ _____ . It may be construed as a regulator of information processing.

    problem solving

   1. The knowledge individuals have about cognitive activity and problem solving, and the strategic steps they take to regulate their ongoing information processing, are called _____ .

    metacognition

   2. There are four steps in problem solving.
     a) First, we have to figure out what the problem is and set one or more goals. This is called problem finding and _____ _____ .

    goal setting

     b) Isolating the correct pieces to the puzzle and working out the general pattern to solve the problem with these pieces is called _____ _____ _____ .

    planning the approach

     c) Taking stock of how the solution process is faring involves _____ _____ _____ .

    monitoring the progress

     d) When individuals feel they have completed their jobs, they are ready to _____ _____ .

    check solutions

Exercises

Self-Review

Circle the letter of the best response.

1. The name of the memory process whereby two pieces of information are remembered because they are associated is
   a. rehearsal.
   b. elaboration.
   c. inference.
   d. recall.

2. One type of inference is called a logical inference. Logical events do not have to be experienced
    a. directly.
    b. deductively.
    c. indirectly.
    d. intuitively.

3. Semantic networks are composed of
    a. chunks.
    b. sensory registers.
    c. prior knowledge.
    d. completeness.

4. Which of the following is *not* a step in information processing?
    a. memory
    b. attention
    c. perception
    d. mediation

5. When you remember someone's address, you are using
    a. recall memory.
    b. recognition memory.
    c. paired associate memory.
    d. redundancy memory.

6. Which of the following processes are *not* responsible for shifting information to long-term storage?
    a. rehearsal
    b. recognition
    c. organization
    d. elaboration

7. The interpretations of words in a book that have more than one meaning are called
    a. extrapolative inferences.
    b. paired associates.
    c. lexical inferences.
    d. hemispheric specialization.

8. The process whereby guesses are made about what might happen in the future is called
    a. spatial interpretations.
    b. extrapolative inferences.
    c. temporal interpretations.
    d. lexical inferences.

9. The process involved when judgments are made about other persons is called
    a. temporal interpretations.
    b. elaboration.
    c. recall.
    d. evaluative inferences.

10. The aspect of perception that does not change with age is
    a. recognition of past events.
    b. differentiation of objects.
    c. need for redundancy.
    d. selection of salient dimensions.

11. Children develop the ability to screen out extraneous noise while focusing on what someone is saying. This ability is known as
    a. active listening.
    b. selective attention.
    c. dichotic listening.
    d. retention.

12. The physical machinery of a computer is known as
    a. software.
    b. hardware.
    c. logic.
    d. fortran.

13. When we attend to a few events in our environment we are displaying
    a. selectivity.
    b. exhaustiveness.
    c. completeness.
    d. conservation.

14. The attention process that requires searching in an organized fashion and exhausting all possibilities is
    a. selectivity.
    b. exhaustiveness.
    c. completeness.
    d. conservation.

15. The interpretation of sensory events is called
    a. inferences.
    b. metacognition.
    c. attention.
    d. perception.

16. When psychologists attempt to learn what children know about problem solving, they are studying
    a. inferences.
    b. metacognition.
    c. attention.
    d. perception.

17. When a task is broken down into primitive steps it is known as
    a. shaping.
    b. a chain.
    c. task analysis.
    d. serial analysis.

18. The programs that guide computers are also known as the
    a. software.
    b. hardware.
    c. logic.
    d. machinery.

19. When certain dimensions are noticed they are said to possess
    a. redundancy.
    b. rehearsal.
    c. selectivity.
    d. salience.

20. The memory used to retain ideas and thoughts as you work on problems is
    a. short-term memory.
    b. long-term memory.
    c. sensory register.
    d. rehearsal.

Comprehension

1. You are a psychological consultant to a school district. You have been asked to develop strategies to help elementary school children remember what they are taught. You are preparing a lecture to be given to a group of third-grade teachers on how memory processes can be used in helping students retain information. List the main points your lecture would include for each of the following.
   a. Rehearsal

b. Elaboration

c. Organization

Application

1. Psychologists have studied memory development by means of a task known as the digit span. With the digit span, several numbers are presented consecutively (e.g., 1–3–5–8) and the subject is asked to recall the numbers in the order that they were presented. Working with a three-year-old, present three consecutive digits and ask the child to repeat them after you finish. On the second trial present five digits, and on the third trial present seven digits. Follow the same procedure with a five-year-old and a seven-year-old. Record all results. Were there differences in the number of digits each child could recall? Did the children appear to use any kind of strategy to help themselves remember the digits?

Answers

Self-Review

1. b	6. b	11. c	16. b
2. a	7. c	12. b	17. c
3. c	8. b	13. a	18. a
4. d	9. d	14. c	19. d
5. a	10. a	15. d	20. a

1. a. There are many ways to rehearse a response. Repeating its name is just one; another is to create an image for the response and rehearse the image. A third way is to employ gestures to repeat an observed response, and a fourth is to create a symbolic code for the response and then rehearse the code. b. When you hear or see something, you may try to remember it by adding to it, or elaborating. In the memory process called elaboration you may associate the experience with something familiar to you, generate an image for it, or develop a sentence or short story about it in your mind. c. Information may be retained by organizing it into smaller units, or chunks, by placing items into meaningful categories, by following the organization inherent in some types of material, by making use of advanced organizers and summaries, and by taking notes or underlining the main ideas.

7 Language Development

Objectives

When you have mastered the material in this chapter, you will be able to —

1. define language;
2. describe and evaluate the old view of language development;
3. describe language learning (interactions of biological heritage, environment, and processing);
4. identify and describe phonological landmarks in language development;
5. describe several patterns of phonological development;
6. describe syntactic and semantic language development;
7. discuss the functions of language and its effects on perception, memory, thinking, problem solving, and communication.

Key Terms

babbling
consonants
cooing
deep structure
echoing
expansion
generativity
grammar
holophrase
Language Acquisition Device
language universals
linguistic competence
linguistic performance
linguistic production deficiency
main language center
mean length of utterance
(MLU)
morpheme

novel utterances
overextensions
phoneme
pivot-open grammar
pragmatics
prompting
psycholinguistics
semantics
surface structure
syntax
telegraphic speech
transformations
underextensions
voiced
voiceless
vowels
Whorf/Sapir hypothesis

Synopsis

I. Introduction
   A. No animal species other than humans can be credited
      with the communication system called

      _____ .   language

   B. The study of language development combines the two
      disciplines of psychology and linguistics, and is thus
      called _____ .   psycholinguistics

   C. From the disciplines of sociology and anthropology has
      come the insight that the social structure of the setting
      in which children learn to talk influences what they say,
      the language rules they learn, and the language rules
      they apply. This perspective is called

      _____ .   sociolinguistics

II. Language: What Is It?
   A. Language is a well-ordered system of rules that each
      adult member of the language community tacitly
      comprehends in speaking, listening, and writing.
      1. Language is made up of basic sounds, or

         _____ .   phonemes

2. The study of the sound system that is principally concerned with the rules used to combine sounds with each other is called _____ .   phonology

3. At the next level is the morpheme, a string of sounds that conveys meaning. The study of the rules used to combine morphemes with each other is called _____ .   morphology

4. The rules for combining words to produce acceptable phrases and sentences are called

   _____ .   syntax

B. A formal description of a speaker's syntactic rules is called _____ .   grammar

   1. The basic underlying idea and organization of a sentence is its deep structure, which may be expressed in alternative surface forms. What is actually spoken or heard is the surface structure.

   2. Since a sentence has one underlying structure and many possible surface structures, syntactic rules explain the different surface forms for a single sentence. These rules are called

      _____ .   transformations

   3. There are other kinds of rules that are integral to language. One concerns the expressed meanings of words and sentences, which has at least two components, the appropriate use of words in social contexts and the appropriate use of words in sentences. These rules are called

      _____ .   semantics

   4. Finally, there are pragmatic rules in every language. Pragmatics concerns the appropriate use of language, with all of its social and physical requirements.

C. A child may know a linguistic rule but be unable to express it in actual speech. He or she may have linguistic competence but fail to evidence it with the appropriate linguistic performance.

III. How Is Language Learned?
   A. The old view
      1. In his classic work, *Behaviorism* (1924), the father of American behaviorism, John B. Watson, argued that language is a complex behavior—complex because its most important representative, the fully formed sentence, consists of a series of stimulus-response associations chained together.

2. This view of language as chains of stimuli and responses lasted a surprisingly long time in American psychology but is generally no longer accepted.
3. The stimulus-response view of language learning fails to explain satisfactorily the child's generativity.
4. Of the many sentences the child produces, a large percentage are novel utterances.
5. Learning theory fails to explain the obvious orderliness, structure, and ever-present rules in children's speech.

B. The new view
1. Experts believe that language learning takes a different form from that described by behaviorists. Although the exact nature of language learning remains illusive, there is general agreement that language is learned as the result of children's active attempts to induce rule systems from the speech that surrounds them.
2. Children are aided in their efforts to induce rule systems. First, the human brain seems especially sensitive to the structure and rules of language. Second, the everyday speech children hear contains abundant information, redundancy, and feedback about language rules. Third, children learn language in order to communicate effectively with others who have mastered it.
3. Evolution
   a) It is clear that our biological heritage is a necessary foundation upon which language is built.
   b) To begin with, language is a skill that evolved. This evolution took place in two phases.
      1) The first was physical evolution. The brain, nervous system, and vocal apparatus changed over hundreds of thousands of years, as humans evolved from Homo erectus to Homo sapiens.
      2) Then came the important second phase, social evolution. Humans, with their newly evolved language equipment, had to create a system for communicating.

4. The brain and physical maturation
   a) The main language center is located in the left half of the brain, in the area of the superior temporal cortex.
   b) Older scientific research suggests that as the child matures, two things happen to the brain that are significant for language: identifiable language centers become localized, and language activity becomes increasingly dominated by the left half of the brain.
C. The role of environment
   1. Just as children's biological heritage is an important factor in their acquisition of language, so also is the environment. Children do not learn language in a social vacuum; they need exposure to a rich supply of speech from others.
      a) Adults simplify speech when they address a young child.
      b) Adults are not the only source of language stimulation for children; children stimulate each other too. Recent evidence suggests that children as young as four years of age can cater their language to the speech maturity of the listener.
   2. Psycholinguist Courtney Cazden has identified three strategies that adults use in verbal exchanges with young children.
      a) In a typical exchange the adult asks a question, the child fails to respond, and the parent follows with a variation of the same question. This strategy is called _____ .   prompting
      b) In another strategy the child says something that is only partially understood, and the adult repeats the understandable portion and calls for more information. This strategy is called

         _____ .   echoing
      c) The child utters a short phrase, and the adult follows it with an expanded version designed to express a more complete thought. This strategy is called _____ .   expansion

D. The child as language processor
   1. In addition to biological programming and environmental input, children also contribute to their own learning of language. Psychologist David McNeill draws an analogy of the child as an imaginary machine, a _____ _____ _____ .   Language Acquisition Device
     a) Linguistic input is fed into the machine. In analyzing the input, the machine is aided by some already existing information about language (knowledge) and some built-in strategies for language analysis (processing strategies).
     b) The result of this analysis is a set of rules (the output) that describe how the input was generated. The rules are then incorporated into the knowledge component of the LAD.
     c) Some nativists believe that the child is "prewired" to detect certain categories.
     d) As the child develops language, the structure of the language processor (LAD) also changes. More knowledge about the structure and nature of language is acquired, and processing strategies gain new efficiency and precision.
   2. A number of psychologists have long speculated that the child's ability to acquire language must also be bound up with general growth of cognitive skills.
     a) Many studies linking Piagetian acquisitions to a variety of language acquisitions have been performed.
     b) Robin Chapman has concluded that there are still problems in specifying the precise connections that exist, due both to the range of ways cognitive skills are assessed in infants and to some of the inconsistent findings.

IV. The Course of Language Development
  A. Phonology
    1. The study of rules used to produce sounds is called _____ . A basic sound is called a   phonology
    phoneme. A phoneme is a class of sounds perceived as identical by speakers of a language.

2. The major phoneme classes in English are of two types, vowels and consonants. Sounds produced by the vibration of the vocal cords as air is passed over them (the air flows through the mouth without being interrupted) are _____ .   vowels
   Sounds produced by interrupting the flow of air somewhere in the mouth cavity and then releasing it are _____ .   consonants

3. A progression in early speech sounds has been observed.
   a) When an infant is born, the only sounds he or she utters that are related to speech are cries.
   b) For the next few months the infant makes sounds we call cooing, vowellike sounds in which the /u/ phoneme appears frequently.
   c) At around six or seven months of age the infant begins babbling. Babbling is marked by strings of consonants and vowel phonemes put together.
   d) Finally, near the child's first birthday, there are single-word utterances.

4. Within a year or two after the first words appear, most of the basic sounds of standard English are heard in the child's speech, even though pronunciation quirks may be evident with some children for several more years.

5. Perhaps the final hurdle the child must overcome, lasting well into elementary school years, is mastery of deep-structure and surface-structure properties of phonological rules.

6. Speech sounds are mastered in a recognized sequence.

B. Syntax and semantics
   1. The child's first words appear one at a time. The term coined to indicate that the child's single word may actually be a whole phrase or sentence is

      _____ .   holophrase

   2. There is no direct means to test the infant's sense of the grammatical content of a specific sentence or phrase, so his or her syntactic knowledge cannot be assessed.

3. The semantic rules are the means by which the child separates the different functions that may be served by the same word.
4. Another component of semantics is how the child uses words to refer to objects and events. The child's first words generally describe active things, like a ball or a car.
5. For words used as nouns, meanings are both overextended and underextended. An overextension is applying a word or term beyond the class for which it is intended. Underextensions are less obvious than overextensions. When a child fails to use a noun to name a relevant event, we may view his or her silence as a hesitation to communicate rather than as an underextension.
6. Roger Brown has identified five early stages of language development beyond one-word utterances.
   a) The first stage begins when the child produces sentences that consist of more than one word. Successive stages 2 to 5 are marked by increments of 0.5 in the mean length of utterance (MLU).
   b) At the beginning of stage 1, the child produces a few two-word utterances. Brown dubbed the speech telegraphic, noting its similarity to a telegram in brevity and information yield.
   c) McNeill (1970) claimed that the child has a grammar, or rule system, consisting of two kinds of word classes, the pivot class and open class, and rules restricting how the classes can be combined.
7. In stage 2 the length of the child's speech increases; the principal accomplishment is mastery of several inflections.
   a) The child learns how to pluralize nouns, specify verb tense, include prepositions, insert articles, include pronominal forms, and so on.
   b) Once the correct form begins to appear in the child's speech, he or she uses it in appropriate places virtually all the time. Also, the order in which morphemes (in English) are mastered is fairly uniform.

8. In stages, 3, 4, and 5 the length of the speech expands, but the major type of change that occurs involves the use of transformational rules: rules that produce negative forms of sentences, questions, imperatives, relative clauses, and compound elements.
9. Beyond the fifth stage described by Brown, the sentences become longer and the child juggles many types of transformations in a single sentence.

V. The Functions of Language
  A. Perception
    1. Language influences the way events are perceived. When a word or a sentence is uttered, the accompanying stimulus events are thereby made more distinctive.
    2. Differences in language habits foster differences in perceptions of the world.
      a) Whorf and Sapir wrote about how such differences between languages lead native speakers to have very different perceptions of the world.
      b) The Whorf/Sapir hypothesis (accepted by few contemporary psychologists in its original form) states that a language with more lexical categories produces perceptions that are more differentiated.
  B. Memory
    1. Memory for nonlinguistic events is enhanced when language is associated with them.
    2. During the latter elementary school years and beyond, children's language techniques become more sophisticated—and more useful—in the service of memory.
  C. Thinking
    1. Language also helps us to think and to solve problems.
    2. Language seems so important in the process of thinking that many people believe it is impossible to think without language.
    3. Vygotsky and Bruner believe that higher forms of human intelligence and thought are achieved because language is developed.

4. Jean Piaget has been the most prominent advocate of the position that thought is primarily independent of language. In his view, language is merely one symbolic means for expressing thought; the original vehicle for the development of thought is sensorimotor activity.

D. Communication

1. Most importantly, language helps people to communicate with each other.

2. As children develop, their ability to communicate improves along several dimensions. They become less dependent upon contextual cues and nonverbal gestures to get their points across. They move out of their egocentric shells, learning to take the perspective of both speaker and listener in formulating messages.

3. Robin Chapman has proposed a developmental sequence of early communicative abilities in children.

   a) In the earliest stage, infants do not use language at all, but gesture and vocalize to express their interest. This stage is called

    _____ _____ .   intentional communication

   b) In the next stage, children use individual words and short phrases to request information, answer questions, acknowledge others, and repeat what they've heard. This stage is called

    _____ _____ .   discourse functions

   c) In the last stage, children use words to play, talk about objects and events that are not present, and purposefully misrepresent reality. This stage is called _____   symbolic

    _____ .   functions

4. The Piagetian concept of egocentricism has been central in the study of children's communication. Roughly speaking, the young child fails to understand that there are two perspectives operating in any communication situation, that of the speaker and that of the listener.

5. Very little is known about the development of children's ability to be effective listeners. It may be that the development of listening skills closely parallels the development of speaking skills, since the person is both speaker and listener in many communicative settings.

Exercises

Self-Review

Circle the letter of the best response.

1. The basic sounds of language are called
   a. morphemes.
   b. phonemes.
   c. consonant.
   d. vowel.

2. The deep structure is the
   a. basic underlying idea of a sentence.
   b. actual spoken sentence.
   c. meanings that words connote.
   d. ordering of words in a phrase.

3. The surface structure is the
   a. basic underlying idea of a sentence.
   b. actual spoken sentence.
   c. meanings that words connote.
   d. ordering the words in a phrase.

4. A holophrase is a word that represents
   a. what a child is thinking.
   b. an underlying idea.
   c. a phrase.
   d. a whole sentence.

5. A vowel sound is produced by the vibration of the
   a. nasal passage.
   b. throat.
   c. vocal cords.
   d. mouth.

6. The hypothesis that states that language influences perception is
   a. deep structure.
   b. Whorf/Sapir.
   c. LAD.
   d. morphology.

7. Sounds that an infant makes that are related to speech are
   a. consonants.
   b. cooing.
   c. cries.
   d. babbling.

8. The rules that relate the different surface structure for a single sentence are known as
   a. deep structure.
   b. transformations.
   c. syntax.
   d. morphology.

9. Pragmatics are rules that dictate the appropriate use of language in
   a. morphology.
   b. semantics.
   c. syntax.
   d. context.

10. Semantics are rules governing the
    a. meaning of words.
    b. sounds of words.
    c. order of words.
    d. grammar of words.

11. The language researcher who views the child as a language information processor is
    a. Flavell.
    b. McNeill.
    c. Chapman.
    d. Chomsky.

12. The left hemisphere of the brain contains the
    a. aggression center.
    b. thinking center.
    c. personality center.
    d. language center

13. Vygotsky believes that higher forms of cognition develop because of
    a. socialization.
    b. growth.
    c. language.
    d. maturation.

14. Syntactic rules describe
    a. grammar.
    b. meaning.
    c. ordering.
    d. sounds.

15. The technique used by parents to facilitate language is
    a. imagery.
    b. prompting.
    c. discipline.
    d. love withdrawal.

16. An example of a holophrase is a
    a. "wanna"
    b. car
    c. boat
    d. tunnel

17. Children at the level of symbolic function will represent
    a. thought in their language.
    b. reality in their language.
    c. future events in their language.
    d. past events in their language.

18. The language rules children create are not influenced by
    a. morphology.
    b. semantics.
    c. maturation.
    d. social structure.

19. The theorist who believes that thought is not influenced by language is
    a. McNeill.
    b. Cazden.
    c. Piaget.
    d. Brown.

20. The five stages of language development were proposed by
    a. McNeill.
    b. Cazden.
    c. Piaget.
    d. Brown.

Comprehension

1. You are on a college debate team and are assigned to debate against the old view of language development. Prepare the main points of your debate.

2. What is it about the biological makeup of humans that allows us to acquire language?

Application

1. Visit a two-year-old child on several occasions and record on tape your conversations with the child. Afterward transcribe the child's statements verbatim and indicate whether each is a telegraphic utterance or a holophrase. Also count the complete sentences. With this data in hand, describe the child's language abilities.

2. Locate a mother with a two- or three-year-old child who will allow you to record their conversations on tape. Try to obtain about thirty minutes of verbal interactions between mother and child. After you have taped the conversations, transcribe them verbatim and score the number of times the mother uses each of the following processes: prompting, echoing, and expansions. Present your frequencies for each category and describe the interactions.

Answers

Self-Review

1. b	11. b
2. a	12. d
3. b	13. c
4. d	14. a
5. c	15. b
6. b	16. a
7. c	17. b
8. b	18. d
9. d	19. c
10. a	20. d

Comprehension

1. The stimulus-response view of language learning fails to explain the child's generativity satisfactorily. The number of stimulus-response chains that would have to be stored may well exceed the brain's capacity to store and retrieve information. Second, mechanisms of learning theory fail to explain novel utterances. Third, reinforcement and imitation do not seem to advance language rules. Finally, learning theory fails to explain the orderliness, structure, and ever-present rules in children's speech.
2. Evolutionary changes in the brain and nervous system have allowed humans to develop an abstract system of communication unique in the animal kingdom. Evolutionary changes have also led to a unique vocal apparatus capable of subtle production and combination of sounds.

8 Intelligence and Creativity

Objectives

When you have mastered the material in this chapter, you will be able to —

1. define intelligence;
2. compare and contrast individually administered tests of intelligence;
3. compare the psychometric and Piagetian views of intelligence;
4. discuss advantages and disadvantages of intelligence testing;
5. describe criterion sampling and discuss its use as an alternative to intelligence testing;
6. discuss the stability of human intelligence;
7. describe genetic and environmental influences on intelligence;
8. define creativity and discuss its measurement;
9. describe two aspects of creativity: originality and flexibility;
10. describe developmental changes in creativity;
11. discuss imagery as a factor in creativity;
12. describe classroom exercises that can be used to foster creativity.

Key Terms

associative flow
Bayley Mental and Motor
  Scales
brainstorming
criterion sampling
crystallized intelligence
cultural bias
culture-fair tests
culture-free tests
divergent thinking
educable mentally retarded
factor-analytic approach
g
institutionalization
IQ
mental age (MA)
Milwaukee Project

multiple factor theory
New Orleans Project
normal distribution
Peabody Picture Vocabulary
  Test
psychometric approach
Raven Progressive Matrices
  Test
SRA Primary Mental Abilities
  Test
standard deviation
Stanford Binet
Torrance Tests of Creative
  Thinking
trainable mentally retarded
Wechsler test

Synopsis

I. Definition and Measurement of Intelligence
  A. Pioneering efforts
    1. The work of Sir Francis Galton in the latter part of the nineteenth century served as the background for the development of interest in intelligence and intelligence testing.
    2. Galton was intrigued by the possibility that intelligence might be genetically determined and could be measured empirically.
  B. Alfred Binet
    1. The first intelligence test was devised by Alfred Binet and Theodore Simon to determine which students in the schools of Paris would not benefit from regular classes and consequently should be placed in special classes.
    2. Although the Binet test was made up of items that tested several different mental capacities, Binet was primarily concerned with the child's general intelligence (g) rather than specific mental abilities.
    3. Binet developed the concept of mental age to reflect the general level of the child's intellectual functioning.
    4. Extensive effort has been made to standardize the Binet test. By administering the test to large numbers of people and recording the results, it has been found that intelligence, as measured by Binet, has a bell-shaped, or _____ _____ .

    normal distribution

    5. The revisions of the Binet tests have resulted in what are now called the Stanford-Binet tests. The Stanford-Binet has a mean of 100 and a standard deviation of 16. (The mean is the average score, and the standard deviation tells how much the scores vary.)
    6. Although the Binet is still one of two major tests used to measure intelligence, it was developed over seventy years ago and its appropriateness for today's culture is questioned by such scholars as Robert Thorndike.

C. The Wechsler Scales
  1. This test, named after psychologist David Wechsler, actually consists of several different intelligence tests.
  2. Whereas the Stanford-Binet is organized in terms of age levels, the components of the Wechsler scales are divided into clusters of different abilities.
D. The factor-analytic approach
  1. The earliest proponent of the view of intelligence as a set of specific factors was C. E. Spearman. His was called a two-factor theory of intelligence; he believed that intelligence consisted of a general factor (g) and a specific factor (s).
  2. A multiple-factor theory of intelligence, such as that developed by L. L. Thurstone, stresses that a number of factors, rather than one general factor, make up intelligence. Thurstone's ideas on the measurement of intelligence are the basis of the SRA Primary Abilities Test. The test consists of five different batteries, ranging from kindergarten to grade twelve.
  3. Raymond Cattell proposed that two forms of intelligence acted to influence the primary mental abilities described by Thurstone. The form of intelligence that focuses on the child's adaptability and the capacity to perceive things and integrate them mentally is called _____ . The intelligence determined by schooling and environment, which involves learned skills and abilities, is called _____ .

fluid

crystallized

  4. Guilford developed a model of intelligence that has been called the _____ _____ _____ . He conceives of intelligence as having three major dimensions—operations, contents, and products—each with several subdimensions.

structure
of intellect

  5. Although many experts accept the idea that intelligence is made up of a number of specific attributes, they also believe that factor analysis reveals nothing about how intelligence develops or how heredity and environment interact to produce intelligence.

E. Vocabulary tests: indicators of intelligence?
   1. Although vocabulary seems to be related to general intelligence, vocabulary tests measure only one facet of intelligence and should not be used in isolation from other measures of intelligence.
   2. The Peabody Picture Vocabulary Test is widely used as a test of intelligence. It was expected to be less culturally biased in the assessment of children from low-income families than other intelligence tests, but children from minority groups actually score lower on the Peabody than on other intelligence tests.
F. Group tests
   1. The IQ scores in most school records come from intelligence tests administered in large group settings.
   2. Group tests of intelligence, although easy to administer and based on well-established norms, should not be used as a substitute for an individual intelligence test, where the examiner is better able to observe the causes of good or bad performance on particular test items.
G. Culture-free and culture-fair intelligence tests
   1. Because the language of most intelligence tests reflects a middle-class white society, many nonverbal performance intelligence tests were constructed. However, subtle cultural biases often enter into performance tests as well.
   2. One of the most widely used culture-fair tests is the Raven Progressive Matrices Test. There is evidence that individuals with more education do better on the test than those with less education, therefore it cannot be called

   _____ .   culture-free

   3. The Chitling Test was developed by Adrian Dove, a black sociologist, as a sarcastic rejoinder to the middle-class bias of most intelligence tests.
   4. So far, test makers have not come up with culture-free or culture-fair tests that are really culture-free or culture-fair.

II. Comparison of Piagetian and Psychometric Approaches to Intelligence
   A. Piaget and psychometricians agree that intelligence has a genetic component and that the maturation of thought processes is critical to understanding intelligence.
   B. The most obvious difference between Piaget and the psychometric theorists is that the latter group is concerned in quantifying mental growth, maximizing individual differences, and seeking to measure them.
   C. Piaget emphasizes the dynamic nature of intelligence and how it qualitatively changes. He is particularly concerned with how new cognitive structures emerge.

III. What Can Intelligence Tests Predict?
   A. Intelligence tests are still a reasonably good indicator of how well the child—at least, the child from a middle-class family—will do in school.
   B. By themselves, intelligence tests are not good predictors of occupational status. They are invariably used most effectively in conjunction with the types of criterion testing recommended by David McClelland.

IV. Infant Intelligence and the Stability of Intelligence through Different Periods of Development
   A. Intelligence tests, usually referred to as developmental scales, have been prepared for infants. One of the most widely used is the Bayley Mental and Motor Scales.
   B. Research has indicated virtually no relationship between infant development scales and intelligence at five years of age. It should be remembered that one of the reasons for this finding is that the components of intelligence in infancy are not the same as the components of intelligence at the age of five.
   C. Based on statistical techniques, IQ scores obtained at two and three years of age are related to (although not strongly related) to the IQ scores of the same individuals even at ten and eighteen years.
   D. There is a strong relation between IQ scores obtained at the ages of six, eight, and nine and IQ scores obtained at the age of ten.

E. Paul Baltes and K. Warner Schaie believe that the decline of intelligence in old age is a myth, that intellectual problem solving of the highest order can continue into old age.
  1. An increase in crystallized-intelligence scores continues to the age of seventy and beyond. A decline has been noted only in

     _____ _____ .   visual-motor flexibility
  2. Researchers have speculated that when a decline in intelligence does occur, it seems to happen suddenly and in the five-year period preceding death.

V. Influences on Intelligence
  A. Genetic Influences on Intelligence
    1. Arthur Jensen examined the research literature to determine the influence of heredity on intelligence.
    2. Studies with identical twins produced a correlation of .82, while studies of ordinary siblings revealed an average correlation of .50. Jensen places the heritability quotient at about .80 for intelligence.
    3. Critics challenge Jensen's conclusions on three points: IQ tests top a very narrow range of intellectual functioning; most heritability studies have not included environments that differ from one another in radical ways; and some say the original evidence reviewed by Jensen is flawed.
  B. Home
    1. New Orleans Project
      a) For this program, mothers and children were from low-income black families living in the central-city area. The program started when the infants were two months old and lasted until they were three years old.
      b) The effects that were hoped for were demonstrated by the mothers and children who came to the center (the center-based model) but not by those who were visited at home (the home-visit model) by an educator called a _____ .   paraprofessional

c) There were virtually no differences in the mother's or child's behavior at the various measurement points throughout the home-visit model. In the center-based model, the mother's competence in parenting was not changed when the child was four or twelve months old, but it was changed when the child was twenty-two and thirty-six months old.

2. The Milwaukee Project
   a) Rick Heber began his experiment by selecting forty newborn babies and their mothers from the worst slum area of Milwaukee. An intensive intervention program was set in motion with the mother-infant pairs in the experimental group with the goal of enriching the child's environment and developing the mother's competency skills.
   b) Periodically during six years the children in the two groups, _____ and _____ , were given IQ tests. The IQ results for the children when they were six years old reveal impressive gains by those in the experimental group.

   experimental
   control

3. Family structure, family size, and sibling order
   a) Children who grow up in homes where the father is absent all or most of the time score lower on IQ tests than do children whose family life includes the father.
   b) Children who grow up in large families have lower IQs than do children who come from small families.
   c) The siblings who score higher on IQ tests than others are _____ .

   firstborns

   d) The quality of interaction among family members may be the most important consideration in the family's influence on children's intelligence.

C. Institutionalization
   1. The negative influence an impoverished environment can have on a child's intelligence is most clearly revealed in studies involving institutions, particularly _____ .

   orphanages

2. The Saltz study of institutionalization and children's intelligence demonstrates the importance of the quality of the caretaker's responsiveness in the child's social and cognitive development. The children who had significantly higher IQ scores were in the
_____ program.   foster-grandparent

3. The foster-grandparents also showed increases in self-esteem from being able to work with institutionalized children.

D. School

1. The Coleman report did not statistically prove that the type of schooling the average American child experiences has anything to do with his or her scores on measures of achievement. However, it did not prove that quality of schooling is unimportant to how well the child performs in school and on measures of intellectual functioning.

2. Greater gains are seen in intervention programs that occur earlier rather than later in the child's life.

3. When the programs are terminated at the end of the preschool years, the gains revealed at the end of preschool are often wiped out during the early elementary school years.

4. Programs that involve the child's family seem to help more than those that do not.

E. Culture, race, and social class

1. Some experts believe that even if it were possible to develop a truly culture-fair or culture-free intelligence test, it is virtually impossible to eliminate _____   cultural
_____ .   bias

2. According to one theory, a teacher who knows a child's IQ adjusts the teaching level accordingly, and the child is thereby influenced to perform at that level. As a result, some states have stopped administering IQ tests to students. This is the theory of _____   self-fulfilling
_____ .   prophecy

3. Cultural backgrounds do affect children's performance on tests of mental abilities.

4. The mean IQ of blacks is below that of whites. Also, lower-class children and adults score lower on measures of intelligence than middle-class children and adults do.

5. According to Jensen, middle-class children essentially learn in a _____ cognitive manner, while lower-class children learn in an _____ way. associative

    a) Associative learning is S-R learning. It requires the child to make little or no cognitive transformation of the stimulus input.

    b) Cognitive learning is a higher, more complex form of learning. The child who learns in a cognitive way must actively transform and change the stimulus input.

6. However, cognitive and associative learning are now always separable. Also, many experts believe that all children, other than perhaps infants or children living in highly controlled or deprived environments, learn primarily in a cognitive manner.

F. Nutritional and biological environmental factors

1. While it is widely known that what we eat affects our skeletal growth, body shape, and susceptibility to disease, we usually fail to realize that it may also affect our level of intellectual functioning.

2. Animal studies reveal that the development of the brain is related to protein intake and that the nutrition of the mother may affect not only the development of her own brain, but that of her offspring's brain as well.

3. Studies also indicate a relation between nutrition and mental development in humans.

VI. Mental Retardation

A. Mental retardation: a label

1. Mental retardation is not some kind of disease; it is a label that describes a child's position in relation to other children, based on some standard of performance.

a) The term that has been applied to children whose scores are between 25 and 50 is

_____ .   trainable

b) The term that has been applied to children whose scores are between 50 and 75 is

_____ .   educable

B. Causes of retardation
   1. The most widely used current classification of the causes of mental retardation distinguishes between organic and cultural-familial causes.
   2. Damage to the central nervous system, particularly to the brain, can produce mental retardation. This damage to the brain may occur during prenatal or postnatal development or as the result of an abnormal chromosome configuration.
   3. Most instances of mental retardation do not have a known organic cause. Such retardation is termed _____ if there is no   cultural-familial
      detectable brain abnormality, the retardation is mild, and at least one of the parents or one of the siblings is also mentally retarded.
   4. It has been estimated that the number of people whose mental retardation is considered cultural-familial represents about 75 percent of the retarded population.
   5. Some experts believe that replacing the impoverished environment of the cultural-familial retarded child with a more enriched one may stimulate normal or even superior intellectual growth.
C. Learning and social interaction
   1. Retarded children learn in the same way that normal children learn, although their level of performance is often lower.
   2. Because mentally retarded children are easily distracted, the learning process should be made as exciting as possible and the environment simplified to minimize distractions.
   3. The parents of retarded children tend to be controlling, do not support the child's independent play, and use praise inconsistently and inappropriately.

4. Some parents' interactions with their retarded child seem to be based on the child's chronological age rather than his or her mental age. Others fail to challenge, treating the child as incapable of any learning or independence.

VII. Gifted Children
   A. A child who is well above average in intelligence or has a superior talent for something is considered

   _____ .   gifted

   B. Terman found that highly intelligent children were well-adjusted individuals who were also superior physically, emotionally, morally, and socially.
   C. Programs for gifted children usually follow one of three paths: enrichment, grouping, and acceleration. Grouping, the most controversial of the three, has produced mixed results.

VIII. Creativity
   A. Definition and measurement
      1. The prevailing belief of experts who study creativity is that intelligence and creativity are not one and the same.
      2. The aspect of Guilford's theory of intelligence that is most closely related to creativity is what he calls divergent thinking, a type of thinking that produces many different answers to a single question. (Divergent thinking is distinguished from convergent thinking, a type of thinking that goes toward one correct answer.)
      3. According to Torrance, creativity is the process of first identifying a problem and then carrying through until the results of the problem solving are communicated. The Torrance Tests of Creative Thinking attempt to measure specific aspects of creativity, but they also emphasize a belief that a general factor of creativity can be measured.
      4. Wallach and Kogan attempted to refine the ability to separate creativity from intelligence, especially in terms of how creative people think.

a) Creative people can generate large amounts of associative content in attaining novel solutions to problems. This is called

_____ _____ .   associative flow

It is facilitated by a relaxed atmosphere.

b) Their research focused on manifestations of the mix in individuals of _____   creativity

and _____ .   intelligence

B. Developmental changes in creativity

1. Developmental changes in creativity are viewed in the context of Piaget's theory of cognitive development; that is, creativity seems to change qualitatively, even as intelligence does.

2. Some commonly held beliefs about creativity, notably that creativity lessens with maturity, are not supported by research evidence. A person is not necessarily less creative as an adolescent or an adult than as a child; rather, an increase in creativity may be expected as newly acquired cognitive skills are mastered.

C. Imagery and creativity

1. One area of increasing interest in creativity is the role of imagery in the development of creative thinking. The use of imagery has been linked with flexible thinking and creative problem solving.

2. In one investigation, children who showed more originality were more likely to engage in simple image analogies than in personal, symbolic, or fantasy analogies.

D. Encouraging creativity

1. One technique that has been effective in several programs developed to stimulate creativity in children involves sessions where a topic is presented for consideration and participants are encouraged to suggest ideas related to it. This is

called _____ .   brainstorming

2. Another useful technique forces children to think about events that might follow an unlikely

occurrence. This is called _____   playing

_____ _____ .   with improbabilities

3. More important perhaps than any specific technique is the need to foster a creative atmosphere in the classroom. However, experts caution against spending too much time on creative activities at the expense of other equally important learning activities.

Exercises

Self-Review

Circle the letter of the best response.

1. A child's level of intellectual functioning is often represented in terms of
   a. mental age.
   b. standard deviation.
   c. mean.
   d. mode.

2. The mean is the same as the
   a. standard deviation.
   b. mode.
   c. average.
   d. median.

3. The multiple factor approach to intelligence is concerned with
   a. environmental factors.
   b. genetic factor.
   c. different factors that comprise intelligence.
   d. single factors that comprise intelligence.

4. The test that is an example of the psychometric approach is
   a. culture-free.
   b. multiple-factor.
   c. cognitive-developmental.
   d. Binet.

5. A test for infants is the
   a. Torrance.
   b. Wechsler.
   c. Bayley.
   d. Binet.

6. Coleman and his associates studied the impact of
   a. day care on social functioning.
   b. day care on intellectual functioning.
   c. schools on social functioning.
   d. schools on intellectual functioning.

7. Rick Heber was responsible for the
   a. creativity program.
   b. Milwaukee Project.
   c. home-visit model.
   d. psychometric model.

8. In Guilford's theory of intelligence divergent thinking results in
   a. different answers to a single question.
   b. similar answers to a single question.
   c. different answers to different questions.
   d. similar answers to different questions.

9. Convergent thinking results in
   a. identity questions.
   b. information-seeking questions.
   c. one correct answer.
   d. many correct answers.

10. One technique used to stimulate creativity is known as
    a. convergent thinking.
    b. divergent thinking.
    c. elaboration.
    d. brainstorming.

11. Playing with improbabilities is a technique used to induce
    a. creativity.
    b. intelligence.
    c. cognitive development.
    d. social development.

12. High-creativity, high-intelligence persons are more likely to be
    a. withdrawn.
    b. popular.
    c. submissive.
    d. happy.

13. The Raven Progressive Matrices is a
    a. culture-fair test.
    b. personality test.
    c. interest inventory.
    d. mental health test.

14. Severe retardation ranges from an IQ of
    a. 25 to 39.
    b. 40 to 55.
    c. 55 to 70.
    d. 75 to 90.

15. Cretinism is caused by a deficiency in the
    a. lymph.
    b. thyroid.
    c. hypothalamus.
    d. thalamus.

16. What appears to decline five years prior to death?
    a. personality
    b. sociability
    c. activity level
    d. intelligence

17. According to Jensen, lower-class children learn in a
    a. cooperative manner.
    b. S-R manner.
    c. associative manner.
    d. cognitive manner.

18. Environmental causes of retardation are known as
    a. Down's syndrome.
    b. trainable-educable.
    c. cultural-familial.
    d. structure-functional.

19. Spearman, Thurstone, and Guilford have studied intelligence from the
    a. factor-analytic perspective.
    b. psychometric perspective.
    c. culture-free perspective.
    d. learning perspective.

20. In whose laboratory did Piaget work?
    a. Spearman
    b. Jensen
    c. Binet
    d. Thurstone

Comprehension

1. You are a high school counselor and have just received the results of some intelligence tests that were administered to your students. How will these test results help you as a counselor? What are their limitations?

2. Compare and contrast the Stanford-Binet and Wechsler intelligence tests.

Application

1. With a group of five preschool or school-aged children try to stimulate creative responses by using the brainstorming technique. Remember, in brainstorming sessions a topic is presented for consideration and all the participants are encouraged to suggest ideas related to it. After the discussion is well started, encourage children to combine ideas that have been presented. For a topic, tell the children that you want some ideas about how we can get rid of pollution. List the ideas that the group generates for dealing with pollution.

2. Perform a mini-experiment on Rosenthal's self-fulfilling prophecy. Create the names of three fictitious children. Attribute an IQ of 80 to one child, 100 to the second, and 120 to the third. Ask at least ten acquaintances what kinds of school subjects they think each of these children will enroll in during their high-school years. Summarize the results of your mini-experiment. Did any of the results surprise you?

Answers

Self-Review

1. a		11. a	
2. c		12. b	
3. c		13. a	
4. d		14. a	
5. c		15. b	
6. d		16. d	
7. b		17. c	
8. a		18. c	
9. c		19. a	
10. d		20. c	

Comprehension

1. Intelligence tests are still a reasonably good predictor of how well a middle-class child will do in school. Intelligence tests also can help in diagnosing a child's strong and weak areas of functioning that relate to reading ability. However, intelligence tests are not good predictors of job performance.
2. The Stanford-Binet is organized in terms of age levels. Binet recognized that intelligence actually consists of many different functions, but these were not individually measured and translated into scores. The components of the Wechsler Scales have been designed to provide specific scores for overall intelligence as well as for the individual functions through which intelligence is revealed. While retaining the idea of general intelligence, the Wechsler Scales approach intelligence as clusters of many different abilities.

Part 3

Social, Emotional, and Personality Development

9 The Socialization Process

Objectives

When you have mastered the material in this chapter, you will be able to—

1. define socialization and social agent;
2. describe and give examples of these socialization processes: reinforcement, punishment, and imitation or modeling;
3. discuss the psychoanalytic, behavioristic, neo-behavioristic, cognitive-developmental, and humanistic and ethological perspectives on socialization;
4. discuss the anthropological and sociological perspectives on socialization;
5. discuss the cognitive components of social learning theory;
6. discuss power and assertion, induction, and love-withdrawal disciplining techniques.

Key Terms

adaptiveness
axioms
behaviorism
culture
defense mechanism
ecological structure
ego
enculturation
ethology
evolution
extinction
goals
humanists
id
identification
impression formation

imprinting
induction
instinct
modeling
neo-behaviorism
organization
Parent Effectiveness Training
political structure
power assertion
propositions
reciprocal determinism
reinforcement
role
role taking
self-actualization
social agent

social cognition
social comparison
socialization
social learning theory
superego
time out
value structure

Synopsis

  I. Introduction
     A. Any person who comes in contact with a child and
        affects how the child behaves is a

        _____ _____ .   social agent

 II. Socialization Perspectives
     A. Many areas of socialization research can be traced to
        psychoanalytic theory, which was proposed by

        _____ _____ .   Sigmund Freud

        1. Freud believed that the development of the
           personality is heavily controlled by biological
           processes. He labeled these processes

           _____ .   instinct

        2. The child is destined to forever deal with conflict
           between the three parts of the personality—the

           _____ , _____ ,   id/ego
           and _____ .   superego

        3. The first five years of the child's life were seen by
           Freud as the critical years in the individual's
           personality development. During these years the
           central theme is _____ . This was   identification
           pictured as the child's way of resolving inner
           conflict and sexual desires for the opposite-sex
           parent by patterning himself or herself after the
           same-sex parent. Thus, identification is a

           _____ _____ .   defense mechanism

        4. Erik Erikson has reworked Freud's theory, placing
           more emphasis on the role of culture and
           experiences.
     B. In behaviorism and social learning theory the child's
        behavior is thought to be shaped by social agents.
        1. In the 1920s John B. Watson developed
           behaviorism into a prominent view in psychology.

118

Watson was critical of those who believed the
child's behavior is dominated by instincts.
2. B. F. Skinner continued the behavioral emphasis of
Watson, working primarily with animals while
liberally applying his ideas to human development.
Skinner believes that looking for internal
determinants of behavior inhibits the search for the
true determinants of behavior.
3. A view of socialization that has behavioral roots
and characteristics is social learning theory,
sometimes referred to as _____ .   neo-behaviorism
Current social learning theories emphasize internal
controls and biological constraints on what may be
learned.
    a) Cognitive social learning theory is a label that
       describes the view of Albert Bandura and
       Walter Mischel.
    b) The child's social behavior partly constructs the
       environment, and the resulting environment in
       turn affects the child's social behavior. This
       process is called _____   reciprocal
       _____ .   determinism
    c) Bandura believes that the child's cognitive
       interpretation of a reinforcing stimulus and
       model provides a more accurate picture of the
       child's social development than direct linking of
       the child's behavior and the reinforcing
       conditions of his or her environment.
C. The application of Piaget's cognitive-developmental
theory to understanding children's socialization
represents a major departure from psychoanalytic and
behavioral theories.
    1. From the cognitive-developmental perspective, it is
       the child's conscious cognitive processes that
       influence the socialization process.
    2. Piaget emphasizes two aspects of any biological
       system. These are _____ and   adaptiveness
       _____ .   organization
    3. Lawrence Kohlberg has expanded Piaget's ideas on
       cognitive development to account for many social
       phenomena.

4. Much of Kohlberg's focus is on children's interactions, while Piaget's writings are mainly concerned with the individual's understanding of the physical world.

D. The humanistic perspective of socialization encompasses a wide variety of views. All agree that the child's personality should be studied with a human, not an animal, model. What should be studied are the child's conscious feelings, ideals, and intentions.

1. This view of the child's personality encourages the individual to reach his or her full potential. The outcome being _____ .   self-actualization

2. The humanistic approach is the least scientific of the approaches discussed. It is based on a cluster of attitudes about how to deal with children, rather than the theoretical components of formal _____ and _____ .   propositions/axioms

3. An example of a humanistic approach is Thomas Gordon's _____   Parent
Effectiveness Training
_____ _____ .

4. Two theorists who have most influenced the humanistic perspective are Carl Rogers and Abraham Maslow.

E. The work of two European zoologists, Konrad Lorenz and Niko Tinbergen, formed the basis for a biological theory of behavior known as _____ .   ethology

1. Lorenz revealed the speed and totality with which young ducklings form rapid attachments to a variety of objects in their environment. He referred to this as _____ .   imprinting

2. Ethologists believe that we can only fully appreciate the origin of social behavior if we recognize that many patterns of social behavior are transmitted through _____ .   evolution

   a) One type of evolution is slow. This is _____ evolution.   biological

   b) Another type is rapid. This is cultural, or _____ evolution.   social

3. Ethologists believe aggression, attachment, and temperament have evolutionary roots.

4. Perhaps the strongest evidence for the role of physical development in the socialization process lies in a series of studies on early and late

maturation. Early maturation generally seems to have positive psychological benefits for adolescent girls, but the results are not quite as clear-cut as they are for boys.

F. Anthropological and sociological perspectives emphasize the effects of existing behaviors, attitudes, values, and products of the group of people who directly or indirectly influence the child. These behaviors, attitudes, values, and products are referred to as

      _____ .   culture

  1. The way in which cultures and subcultures impart behaviors, attitudes, and values to their children is referred to as _____ .   enculturation

  2. Every culture has expectations of what children are expected to do and become. The expectations are called _____ .   goals

  3. In addition, culturally defined rules and dictates prescribe the patterns of behavior that are acceptable for the child.

  4. Family structure, social class, and culture are frequently chosen units of analysis when the sociologist studies children.

  5. The size, density, physical distribution, and social composition of the population form the

      _____ _____ .   ecological structure

  6. The type and amount of material resources form the _____ _____ .   economic structure

  7. The importance of power structures and their subsystems form the basis of the

      _____ _____ .   political structure

  8. Cultural ethics and morals, standards of right and wrong, and rules and regulations reflect the

      _____ _____ .   value structure

  9. A range of actions and a set of functions make up a _____ .   role

III. Social Learning and Cognitive Concepts

  A. Three main concepts have dominated the social learning approach to socialization.

    1. A behavior followed by a positive reward is likely to recur. Such reward is called

      _____ .   reinforcement

a) Studies of reinforcement with nursery school children usually begin with a baseline measure of the behavior that needs to be changed. The second step is often called acquisition, during which time a new response is being reinforced. A third step refers to a decrease in performance when positive reinforcement is removed from the desired behavior. This is called

_____ .   extinction

b) At an early age children are interpreting reinforcing stimuli. Through their growing awareness of others, they interpret reinforcement in a relative sense. This is known as _____   social

_____ .   comparison

c) Self-reinforcement (self-produced consequences for one's own actions) is just as important as reinforcement from others.

d) Socialization is a reciprocal process; whenever one person is trying to control another, there usually is someone resisting control or attempting control in return.

2. A frequent application of punishment in behavior modification has been through the technique whereby a child is removed to an isolated place where there are no interactions with others or any rewarding activities. This procedure is called

_____ _____ .   time out

Most professionals who attempt behavior change recommend the use of time out over conventional punishment.

3. Different discipline practices have been identified.

a) Attempts to gain control over the child or the child's resources by such means as removing privileges, spanking, or threatening are called

_____ _____ .   power assertion

b) Reasoning and explanation of the consequences of the child's actions for others are employed in _____ .   induction

c) Love withdrawal often suggests the removal of the child from the parent.

4. Glasser believes that children should be allowed to determine their own discipline and to set the consequences for their own actions.

5. Punishing the child soon after he or she has done something wrong is more effective than later punishment, when the rewarding aspects of the deviant behavior may outweigh the inhibiting effects of punishment.

6. Everyone learns extensively by example. This form of learning is called imitation, or

_____ .   modeling

7. Bandura believes that several psychological concepts are involved in imitation. One of these is attention; the others are retention, motoric reproduction, and incentive conditions, in that order.

8. Imitation is one of the major ways that emotional feelings and attitudes are learned and eliminated.

B. Many psychologists have emphasized the role of cognitive concepts in socialization.

  1. Mischel has discussed a number of specific cognitive concepts he feels are central to understanding the socialization of children.

    a) The expectancies the child has for his or her own behavior as well as for the behavior of others are important determinants of social behavior.

    b) Children also have the cognitive capacity to generate complex plans.

    c) The manner in which the child processes incoming information and cognitively transforms or encodes stimuli affects his or her social behavior.

    d) The values the child places on a stimulus is an important determinant of behavior.

  2. The subdiscipline of cognitive-developmental theory that is focused on social reasoning is labeled

_____ _____ .   social cognition

  3. The three aspects of impression formation that have received the most attention are differentiation, inference, and organization.

  4. The ability to empathize with or understand the feelings of others is called

_____ _____ .   role taking

Exercises

Self-Review

Circle the letter of the best response.

1. The term *not* associated with Freud is
   a. id.
   b. ego.
   c. imitation.
   d. superego.

2. Instinct is not commonly associated with
   a. mental illness.
   b. behaviorism.
   c. personality.
   d. survival.

3. According to Freud, the first five years of life is concerned with
   a. identification.
   b. object permanence.
   c. discrimination.
   d. generalization.

4. Erikson, in contrast to Freud, is more concerned with
   a. sexuality.
   b. identification.
   c. cognitive stages.
   d. culture.

5. Watson was a prominent spokesman for
   a. behaviorism.
   b. structuralism.
   c. humanism.
   d. ethology.

6. A neo-behavioristic theory is
   a. structuralism.
   b. humanism.
   c. social learning theory.
   d. ethology.

7. Reciprocal determinism is emphasized by
   a. Erikson.
   b. Bandura.
   c. Piaget.
   d. Skinner.

8. Piaget's cognitive developmental perspective is concerned primarily with
   a. observational learning.
   b. attachment.
   c. emotional development.
   d. conscious cognitive processes.

9. Imprinting is generally associated with the theoretical perspective of
   a. ethologists.
   b. social learning theorists.
   c. cognitive developmentalists.
   d. humanists.

10. Parent Effectiveness Training is governed by the philosophical orientation of
    a. humanism.
    b. ethology.
    c. behaviorism.
    d. structuralism.

11. An example of power assertion is
    a. yelling.
    b. ignoring.
    c. reasoning.
    d. spanking.

12. The concept or process involved when children compare themselves with other children is
    a. social comparison.
    b. socialization.
    c. partial reinforcement.
    d. self-reinforcement.

13. The concept or process involved when a child praises himself or herself is
    a. imitation.
    b. discrimination.
    c. generalization.
    d. self-reinforcement.

14. Ignoring a child's requests for affection may be an example of
    a. love-withdrawal.
    b. induction.
    c. power assertion.
    d. time out.

15. Another name for observational learning is
    a. punishment.
    b. shaping.
    c. modeling.
    d. reinforcement.

16. The orientation that weds learning and cognition is
    a. structuralism.
    b. psychoanalytic.
    c. ethological.
    d. social learning.

17. An important component of social learning theory is
    a. self-concept.
    b. scheme.
    c. attention.
    d. equilibration.

18. The process whereby parents impart cultural information to their offspring is known as
    a. socialization.
    b. manipulation.
    c. enculturation.
    d. assimilation.

19. The term that describes a decrease in performance when positive reinforcement is removed is
    a. discrimination.
    b. extinction.
    c. withdrawal.
    d. induction.

20. The study of the development of social reasoning is also known as
    a. shaping.
    b. modeling.
    c. moral reasoning.
    d. social cognition.

Comprehension

1. Why does Bandura assert that a society resembling George Orwell's *1984* may never evolve? Do you agree or disagree with him?

2. How does social learning theory differ from behaviorism?

Application

1. You are going to conduct a survey of at least ten families. At least five of these families are to have children five years or younger. Ask the mother and father of each family what they do when they discipline their children. Write exactly what each parent tells you. Then classify all of your responses into the following categories: power assertion, induction, love withdrawal. Which category was used most often? Did mothers and fathers use the same strategies? Were different strategies used with younger children than with older children?

Answers

Self-Review

1. c	9. d
2. b	10. a
3. a	11. d
4. d	12. a
5. a	13. d
6. c	14. a
7. b	15. c
8. d	16. d

17. c
18. c
19. b
20. d

Comprehension

1. The existence of self-produced consequences and personal standards for performance suggests that reinforcement to control someone else's behavior will not always be successful. Whenever one person is attempting to control another, there usually is someone resisting control or attempting to control in return.
2. Social learning is different from behaviorism in that it is interested in the interplay of cognitive and environmental factors in explaining behavior. Consideration is given to attention and memory processes that are not included in radical behavioristic explanations of behavior.

10 The Family and Peers

Objectives

When you have mastered the material in this chapter, you will be able to—

1. describe the effects of maternal employment on child development;
2. describe the effects of divorce on children;
3. describe the father's role in the socialization of the child;
4. discuss the effects of father absence and father-child interaction on children's social development;
5. describe five dimensions of parenting;
6. describe the role of sibling relationships in social development;
7. describe the role of peers in the socialization process.

Key Terms

associative play

authoritarian parenting

authoritative parenting

child abuse

clique

coaching

control-autonomy

cooperative play

divorce

firm control

independence

laissez-faire parenting

lax control

onlooker play

parallel play

peers

peer sociotherapy

peer tutoring

play therapy

postpartum blues

pretend play

psychoanalytic

psychological autonomy

psychological control

sibling competitiveness

solitary play

unoccupied play

warmth-hostility

Synopsis

I. Developmental Changes in Families
   A. The beginnings of parenthood
      1. When individuals become parents, they find themselves facing a _____ that requires a great deal of adaptation.   disequilibrium
         a) They want to maintain a healthy

            _____ _____ ,   marital relationship

            adult friendships, and possibly continue their careers.
         b) They wonder what type of parents they'll be and if they want to use a different strategy in child rearing than their _____   parents did.
         c) A child will place _____ on   restrictions their lives.
      2. More fathers have become sensitized to the important role they play during pregnancy and increasing numbers are attending

         _____ training.   Lamaze
      3. The excitement accompanying a healthy birth is often followed by _____   postpartum

         _____ .   blues
         a) The mother may be more _____   tired than ever before in her life.

b) _____ may not be aware of or sensitive to these extreme demands placed on the mother.   Fathers

4. _____ on the part of the parents must continue into the preschool years.   Adaptation

B. The middle childhood years

  1. _____ agents outside the family such as _____ , teachers, and other adults play increasingly important roles in the child's life.   Social peers

  2. These years are _____ for many parents because children are neither helpless nor fully independent of parental influence.   ambiguous

  3. Work and _____ are other important themes of middle childhood to which parents must adapt.   achievement

C. The adolescent years

  1. Adolescents undergo extremely difficult physical changes that focus on the development of their

    _____ .   sexuality

  2. Adolescents often are characterized by extreme _____ changes.   mood

  3. Parents often expect school guidance counselors to help their children with _____ development when, in fact, there is evidence that high school students spend less than   career

    _____ hours per year with the guidance counselors.   three

II. Changes in Family Structure

A. Fathers, siblings, other relatives, peers, and teachers generally have not been given the credit that _____ have for influencing the child's social development.   mothers

  1. The _____ bond between mother and infant is viewed as the basis for the development of a healthy personality.   attachment

  2. Kagan predicts that the major result of an emotionally close parent-child bond directs the child toward acceptance of the _____

    _____ .   family values

3. In the United States today, children are spending
_____ time with their mothers.   less
   a) One out of every _____   three
      mothers with a child under age three is
      working.
   b) Almost 42 percent of the mothers of
      _____ work outside the home.   preschoolers

B. Working mothers
   1. Because household operations have become more
      efficient and family size in America has
      _____ , it is not certain that   decreased
      children with a mother who works outside the home
      actually receive less attention than children in the
      past whose mothers were not employed.
   2. In a longitudinal study, boys who experienced full-
      time mothering during the preschool years were
      more _____ competent but also   intellectually
      more ready to conform fearful, and inhibited as
      adolescents.
   3. Mothers now take a larger role in breadwinning
      while fathers are more involved in _____   child
      _____ .   care
   4. The effect of changes in the _____   role
      of women can be different for different-aged
      children.
      a) There is no compelling evidence that
         _____ of the mother outside   employment
         the home has negative effects on infants and
         preschoolers.
      b) Working mothers of school-aged children may
         compensate for their absence by increasing the
         amount of direct _____ with   interaction
         their children when they are at home. Such
         compensation does not always occur, however,
         and when it does it may be _____   guilt-induced
         and result in overindulgence.
         (1) School-aged children, even in traditional
             families, have a greater number of
             _____ _____   socializing agents
             such as teachers and peers.

(2) Research indicates that children of mothers who work are independent, and daughters, in particular, hold the _____ role in higher esteem.   female

c) The picture for adolescent children of working mothers is perhaps the most positive of all age groups studied.

   (1) Daughters are more outgoing, independent, _____ , highly motivated, and score higher on indexes of academic achievement and personality measures.   active

   (2) Both sons and daughters showed more competent social behavior and had a stronger sense of personal _____ .   worth

C. The father's role in the child's social development

  1. Until the 1970s, the father was generally neglected in the study of parental influences on the _____ .   child

   a) _____ theory places considerable importance on the father's role in socialization while other theories have neglected it.   Psychoanalytic

   b) Family _____ have had the most to say about the importance of the father in the child's socialization; they believe the father has a low _____ in the American family for four reasons.   sociologists / status

    (1) It is believed that the father's role had been much _____ than the mother's.   weaker

    (2) There is no _____ basis for the father-child relationship as there is for the mother-child relationship.   biological

    (3) The father is poorly _____ for his parental role.   prepared

    (4) The success of the father's parental _____ depends upon the success of his pair-bond with the child's mother.   role

c) We may gain a better understanding of the father's function by considering nonhuman species where, after procreation, his function primarily involves _____ of the mother and offspring.

    protection

d) Studies of human fathers and their infants confirm that many fathers can and do act sensitively and _____ with their infants and that infants form

    responsively

_____ to both their mothers and fathers at roughly the same age.

    attachment

e) In virtually all of the investigations of fathers and infants, mothers have been the _____ caregivers, while fathers have had minimal caregiving responsibilities.

    primary

f) Lamb found that whether the parent was a mother or a father _____ their behavior more noticeably than whether the family was traditional or nontraditional.

    differentiated

2. Studies of the father's _____ from the home may provide some clue to the importance of the nuclear family for the child's social development.

    absence

a) The increase in the number of children growing up in single-parent families is staggering. Forty to 50 percent of the individuals born in the _____ will spend some part of their childhood in a single-parent home.

    1970s

b) About 11 percent of all American households now are made up of so-called _____ families which include families with stepparents or cohabiting adults.

    blended

D. Effects of divorce on children

1. Stress, conflict, and problems involved in family dynamics predispose children from homes in which the father is absent to be less competent in

_____ and _____ development. Not all of the blame should fall on the family because many people, such as teachers,

    social/cognitive

_____ children from divorced homes to have problems, whether they actually do or not.

    expect

2. Children show a strong desire to live in two-parent rather than one-parent homes, thus _____ is difficult for most children.   divorce
   a) A great deal of upheaval in family functioning occurs in divorced families, producing a state of _____ .   disequilibrium
   b) This period in the first year after divorce is followed by an _____ that seems to stabilize by the end of the second year.   equilibrium
3. Some of the most negative effects of divorce on children may be associated with _____ _____ .   economic problems
   a) Only one of every three _____ contributes to the support of their families.   ex-husbands
   b) Also, many divorced women do not have the training and skills to obtain a _____ .   job
   c) Mother-headed divorced families often must relocate to a poorer neighborhood, which may mean that children will change schools and lose friends at a time when they need some _____ and support in their lives.   continuity
4. Five of the most important aspects of divorce that influence the child's behavior are family conflict, the father's role, the mother's role, the availability of support systems, and the age of the child.
   a) Many separations and divorces are highly charged emotional affairs that enmesh the child in _____ .   conflict
   b) The child's relationship with both parents after the divorce influences the child's ability to cope with _____ . In the first year after divorce, parents tend to discipline the child _____ , to be less _____ , and to be ineffective in _____ the child.   stress   inconsistently   affectionate   controlling
   c) Divorced mothers with custody have more difficulty with _____ than they do with _____ .   daughters   sons

d) Support systems for divorced families seem
more important for _____ -   low
income families than _____ -   middle
income families.

e) Young children may _____   blame
themselves more for the divorce and distort the
feelings and behavior of their parents, including
hopes for their _____ .   reconciliation

III. Parent-Child Relationships

A. The dimension of parenting referred to as
_____ has been the focus of   control
considerable debate in child psychology.

1. The _____ dimension of parenting   control-autonomy
refers to the parents' establishment and
enforcement of _____ and to the   rules
techniques used to promote or hinder the child's
development of _____ .   independence

a) _____ _____   Psychological control
consists of parental behavior that keeps the
child closely tied to the parent, while

_____ _____   psychological autonomy
refers to parent behavior that allows the child
to develop more independently.

b) _____ _____   Firm control
occurs when the parent sets rules and
regulations and requires the child to abide by
them, while _____   lax
_____ results when the parent   control
establishes rules but does not enforce them or
does not develop clear-cut standards for the
child's behavior.

2. The _____ _____   social competency
of children can be influenced by the kind of social
interaction they have with their parents. Three
types of parenting behaviors have been related to
different aspects of children's social behavior.

a) _____ parenting describes   Authoritarian
parents who are restrictive, have a punitive
orientation, exhort the child to follow their
directions, respect work and effort, and place
limits and controls on the child, with little
verbal give-and-take between parent and child.

b) _____ parenting encourages the child to be independent but still places limits, demands, and controls on the child's actions. There is extensive verbal give-and-take, and parents demonstrate warmth and nurturance.   Authoritative

c) _____ (permissive) parenting places low demands, limits, and controls on the child's behavior. Parents take a nonpunitive stance and in general are not very involved with the child.   Laissez-faire

3. _____ in parenting is associated with predictable social behavior in children.   Warmth-hospitality

   a) Overly _____ parents who show little affection toward their children have children who show patterns of hostile and _____ behavior.   hostile / aggressive

   b) Parents who show a high degree of warmth, nurturance, and acceptance toward their children have children who show high _____ and altruism.   self-esteem

4. Parental hostility toward children in some families reaches the point where one or both parents _____ the child.   abuse

   a) For several years it was believed that parents who commit child abuse are severely disturbed, "sick" individuals. Recent research, however, reveals that parents who abuse their children are rarely _____ .   psychotic

   b) Parke's model shifts the focus from the personality traits of the parents to an analysis of three aspects of the social environment—cultural, familial, and _____ influences.   community

      (1) American culture sanctions _____ .   violence

      (2) Many parents who abuse their children were _____ themselves.   abused

      (3) Both family resources and such formal support systems of the community as crisis centers and child-abuse counseling are associated with a _____ in child abuse.   reduction

B. Children may affect their caregivers as much as their caregivers affect them.
  1. The child's level of _____ elicits certain parental behavior.   development
  2. There are rather strong individual differences in children's _____ _____ .   activity levels
  3. _____ differences such as differences in responsiveness may contribute to differences in the way adults behave toward infants.   Temperamental
  4. _____ characteristics of an infant or young child may elicit negative behaviors, such as abuse, from parents.   Deviant

C. Not only should the reciprocal nature of parent-child relationships be considered when explaining the child's social behavior, but also the entire _____ of interacting individuals in the family.   system
  1. If we are serious about studying the entire family system, we must look at all possible _____ and interchanges.   relationships
  2. Hartup believes that the family system provides an affective base from which the young child can explore the wider social world without excessive _____ or _____ .   anxiety/distress

IV. Siblings
  A. _____ among siblings, along with the concern about being treated fairly and equally by parents, are among the most pervasive characteristics of sibling relationships.   Competition
  B. More than _____ percent of American children have one or more siblings.   80
  C. It is usually believed that _____ children tend to be somewhat neglected by parents. Mothers seem more attentive and anxious with their firstborn than with children born later, perhaps causing differences in the children's behavior.   middle
  D. Several recent studies have focused on the interaction of siblings.
    1. An infant tends to look at, _____ , and follow an older sibling about, whereas the older sibling tends to show little interest in the infant.   imitate

2. In studies of sibling pairs, firstborns were more
_____ than the second child,   dominant
although this was moderated by the age spacing of
the siblings and _____ of siblings.   sex
3. _____ close in age were found to   Brothers
have the least harmonious relationships.
4. In some instances siblings are a stronger
_____ influence than the parents.   socializing

V. Peers
   A. Functions of the peer group
      1. To many children, how they are
         _____ by their peers is the most   viewed
         important aspect of their lives.
      2. The term *peers* usually refers to children who are
         about the same _____ and who   age
         interact at about the same _____   behavioral
         level; however, children often interact with other
         children who are three or more years older or
         younger.
      3. Social contacts and _____ are   aggression
         more characteristic of same-age peers.
      4. One of the most important functions of the peer
         group is to provide a source of
         _____ about the world outside the   information
         family. From the peer group the child receives
         _____ about his or her abilities.   feedback
   B. The development of peer relations
      1. Infants as young as six months of age
         _____ when placed together.   interact
      2. _____ seem to be very important   Toys
         to peer interaction during most of the toddler stage.
      3. Positive interchanges, affective displays, and
         _____ interchanges are more   negative
         common in the second year than the first.
      4. As toddlers become preschoolers, their peer
         interaction increasingly involves trading
         _____ rather than objects because   words
         of increased _____ facility.   verbal
      5. Perhaps the most elaborate attempt to examine
         developmental changes in children's social play was
         conducted many years ago by
         _____ .   Parten
         She developed six categories of play.

a) When a child is not engaged in play as it is
commonly understood, he or she is considered

_____ .   unoccupied

b) When a child plays alone and independently of
those around him or her, he or she is in

_____ play.   solitary

c) When a child watches other children playing
but does not enter into the play, he or she is
an _____ .   onlooker

d) _____ play occurs when a   Parallel
child plays alone, but with toys like those that
other children are using or in a manner that
mimics the behavior of other playing children.

e) _____ play takes place when   Associative
there is social interaction with little or no
organization.

f) Social interaction in an organized activity
characterizes _____ play.   cooperative

C. Play

1. When children engage in _____   pretend
play they have transformed the physical
environment into a mental symbol.

2. There are many _____ of play.   functions

a) Play maintains affiliation with

_____ .   peers

b) Play allows the child to work out
_____ and conflicts.   anxieties

c) Piaget sees play as a medium that helps
advance the child's _____   cognitive
development. At the same time he stresses that
the _____ of cognitive   level
development the child has attained may
constrain the way in which he or she plays.

d) Play serves as a means whereby the child can
safely _____ and seek out   explore
new _____ .   information

D. Peer relations and social behavior

1. Studies of the relationship between peer models and
their observers indicate that a _____ positive
relationship with the model and a perceived
_____ between the model and the   similarity
observer enhance modeling. Peer relations are also
affected by the extent to which individuals
dispense _____ to each other.   rewards

2. The _____ system in the United States has not systematically called upon the peer group to the extent that other countries have.

    educational

3. One conglomerate strategy used to help children get along better with their peers is called _____ , which combines demonstration, rational discussion sessions, and _____ .

    coaching

    shaping

4. Being yourself, being happy, showing enthusiasm and concern for others, and showing self-confidence but not conceit are among the characteristics that lead to _____ . Children who are more physically _____ and _____ are also more popular.

    popularity

    attractive

    brighter

5. While friendship is considered a strong need by youth, many lack skills to _____ and maintain friendships, and others are wary of the _____ such friendship brings.

    initiate

    commitments

E. Children's groups

  1. An assemblage of children is not necessarily a group or clique.

    a) A _____ exists when several children interact with each other on an ongoing basis, sharing _____ and _____ .

    clique

    values

    goals

    b) _____ are the standards, rules, and guidelines by which the group abides.

    Norms

  2. Children's groups are usually smaller and less formal than _____ groups.

    adolescent

  3. Family and _____ backgrounds play critical parts in the development of both informal and formal peer groups.

    cultural

F. In times of stress children usually move toward their _____ rather than toward their _____ .

    parents

    peers

G. While parents are not as good at playing with their children as children are among themselves, parents often take an active role in monitoring their children's _____ of playmates and the form of their play.

    choice

H. The child's relations with his or her parents serve as an _____ basis for exploring and enjoying positive peer relations.

    emotional

Exercises

Self-Review

Circle the letter of the best response.

1. The excitement accompanying a healthy birth is often followed by
    a. close ties with extended family members.
    b. less emphasis on careers.
    c. postpartum blues.
    d. a positive marital relationship.

2. The basis for the development of a healthy personality is
    a. strong family values.
    b. a strong attachment bond.
    c. strong religious values.
    d. strong achievement motivation.

3. The percent of working mothers with a child under three is
    a. 33.
    b. 50.
    c. 66.
    d. 75.

4. The effects of maternal employment on development is most positive for
    a. toddlers.
    b. preschoolers.
    c. school-age children.
    d. adolescents.

5. The theory that has placed considerable importance on the father's role in socialization is
    a. cognitive development.
    b. psychoanalytic.
    c. social learning.
    d. ethological.

6. Infants form attachments to fathers
    a. soon after they are attached to mothers.
    b. weeks after they are attached to mothers.
    c. at about the same time as mothers.
    d. only when the mother does not reside at home.

7. About 11 percent of American households now are made up of so-called _____ families, which include families with stepparents or cohabiting adults.
   a. intact
   b. nuclear
   c. nontraditional
   d. blended

8. Some of the negative effects of divorce on children may be associated with
   a. postdivorce adjustment.
   b. economic problems.
   c. maternal employment.
   d. sibling rivalry.

9. The first year following divorce, parents tend to discipline their children
   a. inconsistently.
   b. warmly.
   c. firmly.
   d. rarely.

10. The dimension of parenting that refers to the parents' establishment and enforcement of rules, and to the techniques used to promote or hinder the development of independence is
    a. warmth-hostility.
    b. control-autonomy.
    c. independence-authority.
    d. passive-aggressive.

11. The type of parenting that encourages the child to be independent but still places limits, demands, and controls on the child's actions is
    a. firm.
    b. authoritarian.
    c. laissez-faire.
    d. authoritative.

12. Overly hostile parents who show little affection toward their children have children who show patterns of hostile and _____ behavior.
    a. independent
    b. dependent
    c. aggressive
    d. withdrawn

13. What percent of American children have one or more siblings?
    a. 40
    b. 60
    c. 80
    d. 100

14. Infants tend to look at, imitate, and follow an older sibling about, whereas the older sibling tends to display
    a. dominant behaviors with the infant.
    b. competition with the infant.
    c. affection toward the infant.
    d. little interest in the infant.

15. The term *peers* usually refers to children who are about the same age and show similar
    a. behavioral levels.
    b. physical maturity.
    c. activity preferences.
    d. behavioral responses.

16. During the toddler years, peer interaction seems to center around
    a. toys.
    b. language.
    c. fantasy.
    d. sharing.

17. Perhaps the most elaborate attempt to examine developmental changes in children's social play was conducted many years ago by
    a. Piaget.
    b. Parten.
    c. Bandura.
    d. Furman.

18. When children transform the physical environment into a neutral object they are engaging in
    a. associative play.
    b. parallel play.
    c. onlooker play.
    d. pretend play.

19. Two characteristics of children that are related to popularity are
    a. attractiveness and intelligence.
    b. attractiveness and aggressiveness.
    c. intelligence and aggressiveness.
    d. intelligence and height.

20. The standards, rules, and guidelines by which groups abide is termed a
    a. goal.
    b. norm.
    c. function.
    d. monitor.

Comprehension

1. You are a member of a debate team and your opponent has argued that the father contributes very little to a child's development. Your task is to counter this argument.

2. You are a child psychologist and a married couple asks whether you think the wife's employment would adversely influence their child's development. What points would you include in your discussion with these parents?

Application

1. The purpose of this project is to determine whether preschool girls reinforce each other at play more than preschool boys. For ten minutes observe two or more preschool girls playing together. Then observe preschool boys playing together, also for ten minutes. For each peer group count the number of verbal and physical reinforcers the children give one another.

Do girls reinforce each other more than boys? What other differences did you notice in their play patterns?

2. Some psychologists believe that children spend less time with children their own age than with children who are younger or older than they. Try to shed some light on the controversy by doing a survey. Locate fifteen children and ask them their own ages and the ages of five friends they play with most often. Analyze the results of your survey. Do your results support the notion that children spend less time with children their own age than with children who are younger or older?

Answers

Self-Review

1. c	6. c	11. d	16. a
2. b	7. d	12. c	17. b
3. a	8. b	13. c	18. d
4. d	9. a	14. d	19. a
5. b	10. b	15. a	20. b

Comprehension

1. Discuss in detail the effects of father absence, particularly on the child's role development, and the father's influence on intellectual development.
2. Discuss in detail the evidence put forth by Lois Hoffman that mothers who work do not generally adversely affect their children's development.

11 Schools and Culture

Objectives

When you have mastered the material in this chapter, you will be able to—

1. discuss the socializing role of the teacher;
2. describe the types of education provided during infancy and early childhood and discuss their socializing influence: day-care programs, child-centered nursery schools, and compensatory education;
3. describe Projects Head Start and Follow Through, and discuss evaluations of these programs;
4. compare and contrast traditional schools and open schools, and discuss their socializing effects during middle childhood and adolescence;
5. discuss cross-cultural differences in caretaking practices with infants and their influence on development;
6. discuss some social class differences in parental behavior;
7. discuss the effects of television on social attitudes and behaviors.

Key Terms

acculturation
assimilation
authoritarian teaching
authoritative teaching
child-centered nursery schools
compensatory education
cultural milieu
culture
family day care

laissez-faire teaching
peer pressures
progressive schools
Project Follow Through
Project Head Start
social class
subculture
traditional schools

Synopsis

I. Schools
  A. The nature of the child's schooling
    1. Educators who stress the importance of
       _____ and _____ humanistic/affective
       education believe that schools and teachers should

be working toward developing the child's self-awareness and self-confidence.

2. Open schools, free schools, and alternative schools are labels that have been applied to settings that differ from _____ schools.   traditional

3. Advocates of the back-to-basics movement cite declining _____   achievement
   _____ as evidence that basic skills   scores
   are not being taught effectively.

4. Some education experts believe it is important to have several educational modes to choose from in order to suit the specific _____   needs
   and _____ of individual children.   abilities

5. The dimension of _____ has been   control
   linked to violence in schools. How parents view this dimension of the school system is related to social class.

B. Early childhood education

1. Many different kinds of day-care arrangements have been identified.

   a) In an informal arrangement within the
      _____ , a relative or friend   home
      takes care of the child.

   b) When several _____ cooperate   families
      among themselves to provide day care for their children, the number of children is generally limited to six, with one caretaker.

   c) When an "independent" caretaker provides day-care services in his or her home, there may
      be _____ to   seven
      _____ children and more than   twelve
      one supervising adult.

   d) In a _____   day-care
      _____ , thirteen or more   center
      children are taken care of by several adults in a building other than a home.

2. Day care should include concern for adult-child social interaction, _____   sensory
   stimulation of the child, and opportunities for the child to play and explore the world.

   a) Day-care experts are beginning to develop
      _____ to help parents select   guides
      good day-care centers for their children and to be more concerned about the licensing of the centers.

b) Some experts believe that no distinction should
be made between day-care and

_____ _____   nursery school
programs, while others believe the principal
difference between the two is the amount of
time children attend during the day.

c) Bronfenbrenner concluded that children in the
United States who participate in all-day day
care are thereby disposed to be more
_____ , impulsive, and   aggressive
egocentric than children who do not.

3. Throughout the twentieth century the most popular
form of education for children before the first grade
has been the child-centered nursery school program.
Regardless of the individual variations in nursery
school programs, most are _____   progressive
in their educational outlook.

4. In the 1960s an effort was made to try to break the
poverty/poor education cycle for young children in
the United States through compensatory education.

a) Project _____   Head
_____ was initiated in the   Start
summer of 1965 to provide children from low-
income families an opportunity to experience an
enriched early environment.

b) Congress established Project

_____ _____   Follow Through
in 1967 when it had become apparent that a
program comparable to Head Start was needed
for the early elementary school years.

c) A significant aspect of Project Follow Through
was planned variation; different kinds of
_____ programs for children   educational
were devised to see whether specific programs
were effective with all children or only with
certain groups of children.

d) All Follow-Through programs include
instruction, medical services,
_____ , psychological services,   nutrition
social services, and staff development.

5. A national evaluation of Project Follow Through is being conducted by Stanford Research Institute. Follow-Through pupils are compared with pupils of similar social and _____ backgrounds who have not participated in the project.   **intellectual**

6. A recent national comparison of Follow Through and non-Follow Through programs supported the belief that educational intervention can have a _____ affect on the child's social and intellectual development.   **positive**

C. Organization of schools

1. In one review of the educational practices of _____ _____ versus junior high schools, there were no differences between the two types of schools in teaching strategies, curricula, academic progress, student work load, or _____ activities.   **middle schools**

    extracurricular

2. In one of the few investigations that has compared sixth graders in a middle school with sixth graders in an elementary school, significant differences in _____ development were found.   **social**

D. School and class size

1. Students in small schools engage in a greater variety of activities with their counterparts and hold more _____ slots than students in larger schools.   **leadership**

2. While there is every intuitive reason to argue for _____ classes, there is little empirical evidence to back up this argument.   **smaller**

E. Classroom structure and organization

1. Some education experts have commented that the most significant event in education in the last one hundred years has been removing the bolts that attach seats to the floor, thus allowing children to _____ around the classroom. An interesting study of the traditional seating arrangement indicates that in such an arrangement, the teacher _____ with some students more than others.   **move**

    interacts

2. Structured classrooms are not always associated with better achievement, nor are _____ classrooms always   flexible
associated with better social outcomes. Experts believe a variety of measures should be used to assess the effects of classroom
_____ , and better instruments are   organization
needed to identify the organization in use.

F. ATI: Aptitude X Treatment Interaction
   1. The term _____ refers to   aptitude
academic potential and personality dimensions in which students differ; _____ refers   treatment
to the educational technique adopted in the classroom.
   2. Recent research has shown that a child's achievement level may interact directly with classroom _____ to produce the   structure
best learning and the most enjoyable learning
_____ . Also, successful teaching   environment
varies according to the student being taught. One teaching _____ is superior with   strategy
lower-class students, while another is superior with higher socioeconomic status students.

G. Teacher-child relations
   1. Teacher traits that relate positively to the students' _____ development are   intellectual
enthusiasm, the ability to plan, poise, adaptability, and the awareness of individual differences.
   2. Baumrind indicates that the styles of discipline she discovered in parent-child interaction can be found in teacher-student interaction as well.
      a) The _____ teacher is   authoritarian
dominant and controlling.
      b) The _____ teacher is direct   authoritative
but rational, encourages verbal give and take, and values independence but still admires disciplined conformity.
      c) The _____ teacher provides   laissez-faire
little or no direction and behaves passively.

II. Culture and Cross-Cultural Comparisons

A. The cultural milieu

1. _____ refers to the physical and social setting in which the individual lives. Aspects of the cultural milieu include the institutions of family and school, the structure and function of peer groups, communities and neighborhoods, church, and television and other media.   Milieu

2. _____ , such as Margaret Mead, analyze the cultures to which children are exposed.   Anthropologists

B. The cultural process

1. The label _____ as used here refers to the existing cluster of behaviors, attitudes, values, and products of a particular group of people.   culture

2. There are many _____ within each dominant culture that have their own sets of behaviors and values.   subcultures

3. In every culture there are defined _____ that reflect what children are expected to do and become.   goals

4. It is important to consider whether the child is growing up in a stable or changing culture.

   a) _____ occurs when members of different subcultures interact and the process leads to cultural changes in one or both of the subcultures.   Acculturation

   b) _____ occurs when the members of one subcultural group become completely absorbed into a more dominant group.   Assimilation

5. Careful, _____ evaluation of community influences, cohesiveness and values in neighborhoods, and interactions among the subcultural components of church, community, neighborhood, and family have not been fully explored.   empirical

   a) While different children have been studied in a variety of _____ , rarely has an individual child been observed and evaluated in many different settings.   settings

b) Bronfenbrenner calls for more experiments that attempt to _____ the cultural environment of the child.   transform

c) It is very easy to _____ , using data in a single culture, about the universal aspects of children and their social world.   generalize

C. Cross-cultural comparisons
  1. There are differences as well as similarities between the caretaking of children in the United States and children in other _____ .   cultures

    a) In her extensive work with infants in Uganda, East Africa, _____ _____ observed that infants often cried when they were with their mothers. Her observations of American mothers and their infants, however, indicated that infants smiled in response to their mother's behavior. _____ believes that these cultural differences were due to the fact that the American mothers tried to get their infants to smile.   Mary Ainsworth

    Ainsworth

    b) William Caudill compared the everyday behavior of mothers and their three- and four-month-old infants in Japan and the United States. He found that American mothers chatted more with their babies and that American babies talked more, displayed happier vocalizations, and engaged in more gross motor activity than the Japanese babies. He concluded that the Japanese and American babies had learned different behaviors as a direct result of the different _____ behaviors of their mothers.   caretaking

  2. Many anthropologists believe that the _____ conditions in a culture influence children's social behavior through the child-rearing techniques of parents.   socioeconomic

    a) Barry, Child, and Bacon found that parents in _____ countries place a lower value on socializing their children for achievement and independence.   nonindustrialized

b) Millard Madsen and his colleagues have found that _____ children generally are more cooperative and American children more competitive.

Mexican

c) Wayne Holtzman and his colleagues have found that Mexican children are more cooperative in _____ activities, whereas American children are more competitive.

interpersonal

3. Not only have parent-child relations been studied cross-culturally, but _____ relations also have been the focus of a number of studies.

peer

   a) Beatrice and John Whiting found consistent differences in adult-child and peer interactions across the six cultures they studied. Dependency, nurturance, and intimacy were rarely observed in peer relations but were frequently observed in adult-child interaction. _____ , prosocial activity, and sociable behavior were the most frequently occurring behaviors in peer relations across the six cultures.

Aggressiveness

   b) Children in the United States seem to succumb to _____ _____ more than children in many countries.

peer pressure

4. Except for the _____ taboo, the substance of moral prohibition varies greatly across cultures and is embedded in the values of a culture.

incest

   a) James Garbarino and Urie Bronfenbrenner stress that cultural experiences can be effective in advancing the child's _____ development by increasing the child's exposure to a variety of settings and social agents representing different expectations and sanctions.

moral

   b) Bronfenbrenner found support for this theory by studying children in the Soviet Union; he found that boarding-school students made moral judgments that were more

_____ _____ than those made by day school students.

authority oriented

5. Cross-cultural studies on sexual behavior indicate that culture and _____ play a   learning
major role in shaping sexual conduct. For example, women who live in the Ines Beag culture off the coast of Ireland never have orgasms, while every woman who lives in the Mangaia culture of the South Pacific achieves orgasm.

III. Social Class

A. Differences in ability to control _____   resources
and to participate in the rewards of society produce unequal opportunities for children. Social class, or socioeconomic status, influences how a child is

_____ .   socialized

B. There is by no means total agreement on what the _____ of social class should be and   categories
how they should be measured.

C. The poor are often _____ and   powerless
vulnerable to disaster, have few alternatives, and do not share the prestige, possessions, or experiences of the dominant middle class.

D. Middle-class mothers _____ to their   talk
infants considerably more than lower-class mothers, thereby influencing the variety and frequency of the infant's speech. When socioeconomic factors were
controlled, differences between _____   black
and _____ children were not found.   white

E. The _____ of lower-class students are   aspirations
as high as those of middle-class students; however, when asked which occupation they actually expected to enter, lower-class adolescents mentioned occupations no
more _____ than those of their   prestigious
parents.

F. Teachers have _____ expectations for   lower
children from low-income families than for children from middle-income families.

G. The books children read in school are usually oriented to the experiences and life settings of middle-class rather than lower-class children. More
_____ textbooks would include more of   realistic
the problems and frustrations of lower-class families and more of the frustrations of middle-class children as well.

H. When personality is evaluated in terms of self-concept, achievement, and aggression, there is often a great deal of _____ in the scores of lower- and middle-class children.   overlap

IV. Television
  A. Functions of television
    1. Television has been attacked as one of the reasons that scores on national achievement tests in _____ and mathematics are lower now than they have been in the past.   reading
    2. Television is also said to be _____ , that is, it teaches children that problems are easily resolved and that everything always comes out right in the end.   deceiving
    3. The functions of television are to _____ and to communicate _____ . There has been little concern for the use of television in promoting healthy _____ in children.   entertain / information / development
    4. Aimee Leifer and her colleagues advocate production of more television shows for children that are entertaining but serve a _____ function as well.   socializing
  B. Children's exposure to television
    1. Preschool children watch television for an average of _____ hours a day, and elementary school children have often watched for as long as _____ hours a day.   four / six
    2. Children who frequently use pictorial media are not necessarily frequent consumers of the _____ media, such as books and the nonpictorial parts of newspapers and magazines.   printed
    3. Of particular concern has been the extent to which children are exposed to violence and aggression on television. Up to _____ percent of the prime-time shows include violent acts, with about five such acts per hour. There is an average of _____ times that many violent acts on the Saturday morning cartoon shows.   80 / five

C. Television as a socialization agent
   1. Comstock argues that television should be given
      status as a _____   social
      _____ .   agent

D. Television influence on social attitudes and behavior
   1. Social attitudes refer to the individual's thoughts,
      beliefs, values, and opinions about
      _____ _____ ,   social issues
      including attitudes about minority groups and sex
      roles.
   2. Television affects children's behavior as well as
      their values and attitudes. For instance, television
      violence contributes to _____   antisocial
      behavior in children, particularly aggression toward
      other children. However, television can also teach
      children that it is better to behave in
      _____ rather than in antisocial   prosocial
      ways.

Exercises

Self-Review

Circle the letter of the best response.

1. The compensatory education movement in the 1960s was an
   effort to
   a. change academic policies.
   b. break the poverty cycle.
   c. develop experimental programs.
   d. restructure elementary classrooms.

2. The compensatory educational project that was started for
   early elementary school children is
   a. Follow Through.
   b. Head Start.
   c. Manhatten.
   d. Tennessee Valley.

3. Besides serving children of different ages, Follow Through
   emphasizes
   a. educational materials.
   b. classroom organization.
   c. planned variation.
   d. educational philosophy.

4. Students differ along the dimension of academic and personality
    a. traits.
    b. interaction.
    c. treatment.
    d. aptitude.

5. Students in small schools
    a. do less well academically.
    b. receive an inferior education.
    c. hold more leadership positions.
    d. are less involved in activities.

6. Academic potential is termed
    a. aptitude.
    b. intelligence.
    c. treatment.
    d. motivation.

7. The teaching strategy that is dominant and controlling is
    a. laissez-faire.
    b. authoritarian.
    c. authoritative.
    d. hostile.

8. Anthropologists are responsible for much of the interest in
    a. the education of white middle-class children.
    b. cross-cultural studies of children.
    c. curriculum and teaching methods.
    d. humanistic and affective education.

9. The term used to describe what happens when members of different subcultures interact and the process that leads to cultural changes in one or both of the subcultures is
    a. assimilation.
    b. ethnocentrism.
    c. conversion.
    d. acculturation.

10. What occurs when the members of one subcultural group become completely absorbed into a more dominant group is termed
    a. assimilation.
    b. ethnocentrism.
    c. conversion.
    d. acculturation.

11. When village Mexican children have been compared with Anglo-American children, researchers have consistently found that
    a. American children are more aggressive.
    b. American children are more cooperative.
    c. Mexican children are more cooperative.
    d. Mexican children are more competitive.

12. Mary Ainsworth observed that East African infants tend to
    a. exhibit more positive emotions than American babies.
    b. cry less often than American babies.
    c. cry often when with their mothers.
    d. cry very seldom when with their mothers.

13. American mothers try to get their infants to smile, whereas East African mothers
    a. pay no attention to their infants.
    b. chat more with their infants.
    c. respond less quickly to their infants' cries.
    d. respond more quickly to their infants' cries.

14. Barry, Child, and Bacon found that parents place a lower value on socializing their children for achievement in countries that are
    a. underdeveloped.
    b. agrainian.
    c. industrialized.
    d. nonindustrialized.

15. Wayne Hoffman and his colleagues found Mexican-American children to be more
    a. outgoing.
    b. inhibited.
    c. cooperative.
    d. competitive.

16. Preschool children watch television an average of
    a. two hours a day.
    b. four hours a day.
    c. six hours a day.
    d. eight hours a day.

17. Children who frequently use pictorial media are not necessarily frequent consumers of
    a. printed media.
    b. radio.
    c. motion pictures.
    d. libraries.

18. Social attitudes refer to the individual's thoughts, beliefs, values, and openness about
    a. free speech.
    b. morals.
    c. social issues.
    d. minority groups.

19. Comstock argues that television should be given status as a
    a. entertainer.
    b. babysitter.
    c. social agent.
    d. caretaker.

20. What percent of prime time shows contain violent acts?
    a. 20
    b. 40
    c. 60
    d. 80

Comprehension

1. Should the government continue to provide funds for Project Follow Through? Present an argument for or against the continuation of government funding for this compensatory education project. Base your argument on information presented in this chapter.

2. Anthropologists have argued that children's behavior varies from one culture to another in ways that individuals would have difficulty recognizing if they had experience only with their own culture. Provide support for this argument by documenting cultural variations in parenting practices.

Application

1. Many different kinds of day-care arrangements have been identified. The major concern about day care is that the facilities should provide more than simple custodial care for children. Visit a local day-care center and note how the center concerns itself with (1) nutrition, (2) health and safety, (3) child-caretaker relationships, (4) peer relationships, (5) play, exploration, and problem solving, (6) language development, (7) motor development, (8) coordination of home and day-care center, (9) physical environment, and (10) sex-role socialization.

2. Preschool children watch television an average of four hours a day and elementary school children watch for as long as six hours a day. How much television do children in your community watch each day? Ask the parents of fifteen children how many hours a day their children watch television. Also ask them whether there are any programs that they do not allow their children to watch. Record the results of your survey.

Answers

Self-Review

1. b	11. c
2. a	12. c
3. c	13. d
4. a	14. d
5. c	15. c
6. a	16. b
7. b	17. a
8. b	18. c
9. d	19. c
10. a	20. d

1. Your answer should include mention of the work of Jane Stallings, which indicates that Project Follow Through enhances social development, and the fact that children in Follow Through classrooms tend to work more independently and cooperatively. The long-term effects beyond the third grade have not been demonstrated. Evidence in many educational intervention projects indicates that when treatment stops the gains eventually wash out.

2. Mary Ainsworth observed that the caretaking practices of American mothers and East African mothers differed. William Caudill found similar differences between American and Japanese mothers. Barry, Child, and Bacon revealed that the child-rearing practices of parents in industrialized countries differed from those in nonindustrialized countries.

12 Attachment, Independence, and the Development of the Self

Objectives

When you have mastered the material in this chapter, you will be able to—

1. define attachment and discuss its development;
2. compare and contrast three theories of attachment;
3. define situational variables and detail their influence on the study of attachment;
4. discuss Erikson's views of autonomy;
5. discuss Ausubel's theory of autonomy;
6. discuss adolescent autonomy;
7. discuss the development of the self in infancy, early childhood, and during the elementary school years;
8. define self-concept and self-esteem;
9. differentiate identity, identity diffusion, identity crisis, and identity confusion, describing each from Erikson's viewpoint.

Key Terms

attachment
attachment bond
attribution theory
authoritarian
autonomy
disatellization
ethology
executor responses
identity
identity crisis
insecurely attached infants
longitudinal study
object permanence

overevaluation
rejection
resatellization
satellization
securely attached infants
self-concept
self-esteem
separation anxiety
separation-individuation
signaling responses
stranger anxiety
Strange Situation Test

Synopsis

I. Attachment
  A. A relationship between two individuals, wherein each feels strongly about the other and acts to ensure the continuation of the relation, is _____ .   attachment
    1. The infant tries to maintain contact by crying, clinging, pulling, or shifting locations.
    2. The infant may protest departure by evidencing distress. This has been referred to as

       _____ _____ .   separation anxiety
    3. Crying, clinging to the caregiver, and moving away from and averting the gaze of a stranger are signs of _____ _____ .   stranger anxiety
  B. Research interest in attachment can be traced to work in comparative psychology and to psychoanalytic conceptions of development.
    1. The most comprehensive account of attachment is that of _____   John
       _____ . He has set forth a   Bowlby
       theoretically elegant and eclectic account of attachment based on a synthesis of several traditions in psychology with

       _____ .   ethology

       a) In his view, the infant and mother instinctively trigger each other's behavior to form an

          _____ _____ .   attachment bond

162

b) Bowlby has classified attachment into two main classes of action.
   (1) Clinging, following, sucking, and physical approach are _____ _____ .

   executor responses

   (2) Smiling, crying, and calling are

   _____ _____ .

   signaling responses

c) The development of attachment as an integrated system of behaviors occurs in four phases during the first year of life.
   (1) From birth to two or three months, the infant directs his or her attachment to human figures on the basis of an instinctual bias.
   (2) From three to six months, attachment focuses on one figure.
   (3) From six to nine months, the intensity of attachment to the mother increases.
   (4) From nine months to one year the elements of attachment previously mentioned become integrated into a mutual system of attachment to which the infant and mother both contribute.

2. Mary Ainsworth has offered a number of ideas to the concept of attachment.
   a) It is important to distinguish between an underlying attachment system and overt attachment behaviors.
   b) There are vast individual differences in the patterning of caregiver-infant interactions.
   c) The resulting attachment seems to fall into distinct categories that are relatively enduring for the child.

3. The principal difference between a strict ethological and a strict psychoanalytic account of attachment resides in the structures and mechanisms invoked.
   a) In the psychoanalytic view, the infant invests the primary caregiver with emotional feeling, because she or he is the source of most pleasure. In Freud's word the infant

   _____ .

   cathects

b) The attachment develops as the infant shifts
from radically, self-centered narcissism at birth
to a recognition that others are necessary to
satisfy his or her needs. This recognition is an
early indicator of the _____ .   ego

   4. Learning theorists and cognitive theorists have
explanations of attachment, but these have not been
significant in stimulating scientific inquiry.

   5. Each theoretical approach has provided a useful
addition to the notion of attachment as a whole.

C. Techniques used to measure attachment range from
asking mothers in an interview or questionnaire whether
or not their infants exhibit particular behaviors to
observing videotapes of infants interacting with an adult
in a laboratory setting.

   1. Proximity-maintaining behavior and physical
contact have frequently been measured in a number
of contexts, employing a procedure developed by
Mary Ainsworth, referred to as the

_____ _____   Strange Situation
_____ .   Test

   2. A number of methodological critiques have
surfaced in the past decade, suggesting that the
measure of attachment in infants has not been
adequately observed, or that even when adequately
observed, scientific verification is difficult.

D. There are a variety of empirical sources of evidence on
the development of attachment.

   1. Schaffer and Emerson followed sixty Scottish
infants from age five to twenty-three weeks at the
outset of the study until they were eighteen months
old. This type of study is _____ .   longitudinal

   2. In another well-known study of infant attachment,
Mary Ainsworth observed twenty-nine infant-
mother pairs in Uganda, East Africa, for a period
of nine months.

   3. In a third major effort, Coates, Anderson, and
Hartup observed the same infants at ten months
and at fourteen months, and another group of
infants at fourteen months and at eighteen months.

   4. Although the psychoanalytic view emphasized the
mother as the usual single caregiver with whom the
infant becomes bonded, a consistent finding in

literature is that attachment is quite frequently directed toward more than one caregiver who is around the infant.
E. There are striking individual differences among infants.
  1. The question of the source of individual differences has stimulated much research.
    a) One widely held hypothesis is that differences in the rate of attachment development reflect corresponding differences in the rate of cognitive development. In order to achieve a strong emotional bond with significant caregivers, the infant must first perceive

    _____ _____ .   object permanence
    b) Individual differences in the temperament of mother and child may also contribute to differences in the way attachment develops.
F. Attachment behaviors can be affected by situational variables. The mother's behavior, location of the infant in relation to the mother, and the behavior of the stranger all influence stranger anxiety.

II. Independence
  A. Infants are highly active explorers of their environments.
    1. Ainsworth, Bell, and Stayton judged those children who alternated between pleasurably exploring their environments and calmly seeking their mothers in an unstressed manner to be _____   securely
       _____ . Infants in each of the   attached
       insecurely attached groups had trouble exploring.
    2. Joffe found that secure infants engaged in exploratory activity more than insecure infants.
  B. Margaret Mahler, Erik Erikson, and David Ausubel all have focused considerable attention on the child's push for independence from his or her parents.
    1. Mahler believes that the child acquires a sense of separateness along with a sense of relatedness to the world through the process of

       _____ _____ .   separation-individuation

    The development of individuation has the subphases of differentiation, practicing, reapproachment, and consolidation of individuality.

2. Erikson believes that if the child does not develop a sense of self-control and free will during the second stage of his theory, the child may become saddled with a lasting propensity for doubt and shame. Thus, the goal of this stage is

_____ .   autonomy

3. David Ausubel believes that as children develop cognitively, they begin to realize they are not completely autonomous from their parents, and that this perception can lead to a crisis of self-esteem.

   a) If the child gives up a sense of self-power for the time being and accepts dependence, then the conflict is resolved through

      _____ .   satellization

   b) Two parenting styles that do not produce satellization are _____ and   overevaluation

      _____ .   rejection

   c) As the child approaches adolescence, he or she breaks away and becomes independent through _____ .   desatellization

   d) The process by which the individual's parents are replaced by other individuals or a group is called _____ .   resatellization

C. A series of studies designed to explore in greater detail the young child's development of independence found that the infant's exploration of the environment is affected by both its physical and social characteristics.

D. It is clear that adolescent autonomy is not a unitary personality dimension that consistently comes out in all behaviors.

  1. The adolescent's autonomy is influenced by a variety of social agents, particularly parents and

    _____ .   peers

  2. Studies on the relation between parental attitudes and the adolescent's development of autonomy indicate that adolescents show little autonomy if parents adopt decision-making strategies that are

    _____ .   authoritarian

III. The Self, Self-Evaluation, and Identity
  A. Children begin the process of developing a sense of self
     by learning to distinguish themselves from others. This
     occurs during _____ .   infancy
  B. Children as young as three years of age have a basic
     idea that they have a private self to which others do not
     have access, and by four years of age they distinguish
     this inner self from their bodily, or outer, self.
  C. Maccoby believes that the increasing ability of the child
     to understand how he or she is viewed by others is an
     important part of the child's development of

     _____ .   self-concept

  D. McCandless and Evans believe that important
     developmental changes in self-concept occur as the child
     matures into an adolescent and as the young adolescent
     matures into an older adolescent. Adolescents have a
     more differentiated, individuated, and stable view of
     themselves than they did as children.
  E. The self is discussed in several theoretical perspectives.
     1. Mischel and Bandura, two behaviorally oriented
        psychologists, have had the most to do with
        "putting the self back into the child" from a social-
        learning perspective.
     2. From the humanistic view, the self is viewed not as
        a static entity nor as a personality trait, but rather
        as an organizing principle that governs the child's
        experience.
  F. One aspect of the child's self-evaluation that is closely
     linked with self-concept is _____ .   self-esteem
     1. One method that has been used frequently to
        measure self-esteem is the Piers-Harris Scale,
        which consists of eighty items designed to measure
        the youth's overall self-concept.
     2. Some assessment experts believe that a combination
        of several methods should be used in measuring
        self-concept.
     3. Many studies indicate a positive correlation
        between the child's concept of self and different
        measures of achievement and school performance.

G. Identity is an integrative concept that is used to capture
the diverse, complex components of the adolescent's
personality development.
   1. The term applied to someone of any age who feels
a loss of identity or self-image is

_____ _____ .   identity crisis

   2. Identity confusion may account for the large
number of adolescents who run away from home,
drop out of school, quit their jobs, stay out all
night, or assume bizarre behavior.

Exercises

Self-Review

Circle the letter of the best response.

1. The Strange Situation is used to examine
    a. attachment.
    b. anxiety.
    c. affiliation.
    d. admiration.

2. Ainsworth studied mother-infant attachment in
    a. Turkey.
    b. Mexico.
    c. Uganda.
    d. USA.

3. It has been hypothesized that the ability to form attachments
    is dependent upon
    a. seriation.
    b. conservation of mass.
    c. conservation of weight.
    d. object permanence.

4. Psychoanalytic theory suggests that infants bond with
    a. one caregiver.
    b. two caregivers.
    c. three caregivers.
    d. four caregivers.

5. In an attachment experiment, the behavior of the mother is said to be a
    a. confound.
    b. constant.
    c. situational variable.
    d. matching variable.

6. Children who are securely attached are more likely to exhibit
    a. stranger anxiety.
    b. exploratory behavior.
    c. identity problems.
    d. matching variable.

7. Two parenting styles, overevaluation and rejection, do not seem to produce
    a. independence.
    b. satellization.
    c. attachment.
    d. hyperactivity.

8. According to Erickson, in order to overcome shame and doubt the child needs
    a. self-control.
    b. independence.
    c. anxiety.
    d. self-confidence.

9. Authoritarian decision-making strategies by parents can be related to a lack of
    a. ego formation.
    b. identity.
    c. role taking.
    d. autonomy.

10. By age three children believe they possess a
    a. private self.
    b. superego.
    c. conscious.
    d. conflict.

11. The social learning theorists who study the self are
    a. Skinner and Patterson.
    b. Rosenthal and Zimmerman.
    c. Brody and Stoneman.
    d. Bandura and Mischel.

12. Carl Rogers founded
    a. behavior modification therapy.
    b. Adlerian therapy.
    c. psychoanalytic therapy.
    d. client-centered therapy.

13. Radical behaviorists avoid the concept of
    a. reinforcer.
    b. self.
    c. punisher.
    d. cues.

14. Bowlby bases his work on the theoretical orientation of
    a. humanism and psychoanalytic theory.
    b. ethology and psychoanalytic theory.
    c. operant psychology and social learning theory.
    d. social learning theory and humanism.

15. Attachment becomes focused on the primary caregiver during
    a. one to two months.
    b. two to three months.
    c. three to six months.
    d. four to seven months.

16. Clinging, following, sucking, and physical approach are
    a. discriminative stimuli.
    b. executor responses.
    c. signaling responses.
    d. reinforcement.

17. Smiling, crying, and calling are
    a. discriminative stimuli.
    b. executor responses.
    c. signaling responses.
    d. reinforcement.

18. John Bowlby has presented the most comprehensive account of
    a. prosocial behavior.
    b. aggression.
    c. morality.
    d. attachment.

19. Crying and clinging to the caregiver and averting the gaze of others are signs of
    a. stranger anxiety.
    b. separation protest.
    c. attachment.
    d. affiliation.

20. The study conducted by Schaffer and Emerson in which they followed sixty Scottish infants from ages five to eighteen months is called a
    a. correlational study.
    b. short-term study.
    c. longitudinal study.
    d. cross-sectional study.

Comprehension

1. Several theories for the development of attachment are presented in this chapter. Select the theory that you think explains this phenomenon best, briefly state its main points, and discuss why you think its explanation is better than the others.

2. Design a study to assess whether six-month-old infants are more attached to their mothers than one-year-old infants. Be sure to incorporate the indicators of attachment presented in this chapter.

Application

1. Assess whether children of different ages display attachment toward their mothers. Go to a supermarket or department store and observe young children with their mothers. Summarize your observations. Did the children stay in physical proximity to their mothers? Did the children show any signs of distress when the mother wandered off to shop? Did the children show any signs of distress when they were approached by strangers?

Answers

Self-Review

1. a	11. d
2. c	12. d
3. d	13. b
4. a	14. b
5. c	15. c
6. b	16. b
7. b	17. c
8. a	18. d
9. d	19. a
10. a	20. c

Comprehension

1. Present an overview of the major theories—ethological, psychoanalytic, learning, and cognitive—and then state your opinion of which is best. Be sure to provide justifications for your choice.
2. Your study might include observation of six-month-old infants with their mothers. It should provide for observation of the following indicators of attachment: proximity seeking, fear of strangers, and separation protest.

13 Sexual and Moral Development

Objectives

When you have mastered the material in this chapter, you will be able to —

1. describe how biological forces affect sex-role development;
2. identify sex-role stereotypes, and distinguish these from actual differences between the sexes;
3. discuss the role of cognition in sex-role development;
4. list and describe three aspects of moral development;
5. discuss the stages of moral reasoning described by Piaget;
6. compare and contrast cognitive-developmental and social-learning approaches to moral development.

Key Terms

altruistic
androgen
androgyny
critical periods
gender identity
guilt
hidden curriculum
hormones
imminent justice
instrumental competence

learned helplessness
moral autonomy
moral competence
moral development
moral performance
moral realism
person permanence
role-taking skills
sex role
values clarification

Synopisis

I. Sex-Role Development
   A. Androgyny and the components of sex-role development
      1. The label used to describe differences in children because of their sex is _____ _____ .

            sex role

      2. The extent to which a child actually takes on as part of his or her personality the behaviors and attitudes associated with either the male or female role is the child's _____ _____ .

            gender identity

3. Spence advocates classifying those who score high on both the feminine and masculine scales as

_____ .   androgynous

B. Biological forces, cognitive factors, and development
   1. Biological forces
      a) One of Freud's basic assumptions is that human behavior and history are related to reproductive processes. From this assumption arises the belief that sexuality is essentially unlearned and

_____ .   instinctual

      b) Erikson argues that because of genital structure, males are more intrusive and aggressive, while females are inclusive and passive. This view is the doctrine of _____   anatomy

_____ _____ .   is destiny

      c) Hormones are important in sex-role development.
         (1) Ehrhardt studied the children of women who had received the male hormone androgen to help them avoid miscarriage. Fetally androgenized girls tended to expend more energy in their play and seemed to prefer boys over girls as playmates; boys tended to engage in rough-and-tumble play and outdoor sports activities.
         (2) The high energy level and activity levels of the androgenized girls and boys may be due to the cortisone treatment rather than the androgen.
      d) John Money sees sex-role development as affected by both biology and culture. His ideas are based on brief times in a person's life when biological changes combine with environmental events to produce a virtually irreversible sex-role patterning. These times are _____   critical

_____ .   periods

         (1) During the first critical period (the first three years of life), the child exercises his or her newly formed ability to discriminate anatomical sex differences and simple conventions and to associate these with social attitudes about what "boys" and "girls" are like.

(2) During the second critical period (puberty) the child experiences rapid physiological changes and becomes able to deal with abstract social possibilities.

2. Cognitive factors and development
    a) In order to have an idea of what is masculine and what is feminine, Kohlberg asserts, the child has to be able to categorize objects and behaviors into these two groups. The categories become relatively stable for a child by the age of six.
    b) The child who has acquired the ability to categorize strives toward consistency between use of the categories and actual behavior.
    c) Block believes that sex-role development is a component of a more general personality structure, the _____ .   ego
    d) By the time children are three years of age, they know the sex stereotypes for toys, games, household objects, clothing, and work.
    e) During the three- to seven-year-old age period, children begin to acquire an understanding of gender constancy and increasingly enjoy being with same-sex peers.
    f) In middle-childhood, children increase their understanding of culturally defined expectations for male and females, and simultaneously the behavior and attitude of boys increasingly reflects masculine sex-typing.
    g) With the onset of puberty, interest in the opposite sex becomes more open, although many adolescents find sex a difficult topic to discuss.

C. Environmental influences
    1. Parents, by action and example, influence their child's sex-role development.
        a) Fathers are more exacting and demanding with children than mothers; and whether or not they have influence on them, fathers are more involved in socializing sons than daughters.
        b) A psychologically dominant, powerful adult fosters greater imitation than a submissive, weak adult. A parent who rewards and nurtures the child also fosters imitation.

c) When the dominant adult is of the same sex as the child, strong role development occurs along appropriate sex lines.
2. The feedback a teacher gives boys and girls can significantly influence their sex-typed behaviors.
   a) Preschool teachers tend to respond with reprimands to boys more often than girls.
   b) Female teachers reinforce feminine behavior most of the time.
3. Children and adolescents watch an average of three to five hours of television everyday.
   a) According to more than twenty studies of television exposure since the 1950s, the sex disproportionately presented is

   _____ .   male
   b) Men are also pictured in a greater variety of occupations than women, as well as having higher-status jobs.
   c) In a study on media and career development, students stated that they preferred the occupation depicted by the model of their sex.
D. Sex differences and stereotypes
   1. Mischel defines sex-role stereotypes as broad categories that reflect our impressions about people, events, and ourselves.
   2. Actual sex differences revealed by research are these: boys are better in math, display more aggression, and excel in visual-spatial reasoning, and girls excel in verbal ability.
   3. Two persistent myths about the sexes that are completely unsupported by research are that girls are more social than boys and that girls are more suggestible than boys.
E. Sex differences in achievement
   1. Few topics have generated more controversy in the last decade than the belief that many women have been socialized to assume roles of incompetency rather than competency.
   2. In a review of the achievement orientation of females, females had lower expectations for success across many different tasks than males, lower levels of aspiration, more anxiety about failure, less

willingness to risk failure, and more feelings of
personal responsibility when failure occurred.

3. When a female child believes that the rewards she
receives are beyond her personal control, a state of
_____ _____   learned helplessness
exists.

II. Moral Development
   A. Moral development concerns rules and conventions about
what people should do in their interactions with other
people.
   B. Moral thought, how the child reasons or thinks about
ethical issues, has been researched by Piaget and
Kohlberg.
     1. Piaget concluded that there are two stages of moral
thought. The more primitive one is associated with
younger children: it is _____   moral
_____ . The more advanced one   realism
is associated with older children: it is

_____ _____ .   moral autonomy

       a) The moral realist judges the rightness or
goodness of behavior by considering the
consequences of behavior, not the intentions of
the actor. The moral realist also believes that all
rules are unchangeable and are handed down by
all-powerful authorities.
       b) The moral autonomist accepts change and
recognizes that rules are convenient, socially
agreed-upon conventions.
       c) A third characteristic is the moral realist's belief
in imminent justice—if a rule is broken,
punishment will be meted out immediately.
     2. Kohlberg has elaborated on Piaget's two stages and
characterized moral thought as developing in six
distinct stages.
     3. For both Piaget and Kohlberg, the child's moral
orientation is an outgrowth of cognitive development
that unfolds as a consequence of the interaction of
genetic endowment and social experiences.
     4. Piaget and Kohlberg both believe that peer
interaction is of major importance in the social
stimulation that challenges the child to change his
or her moral orientation.

5. For Piaget, the cognitive processes most instrumental in advancing the child from moral realism to moral autonomy are egocentrism and realism. Kohlberg stresses the importance of information-processing skills for developing more advanced morality inasmuch as these help the child to piece together his or her social experiences.

6. In evaluating Piaget's ideas about moral development, experts find that (1) children generally do go through the stage of moral realism before they reach moral autonomy, (2) moral development is related to intelligence inasmuch as children's general reasoning is a part of their moral decisions, and (3) the change from realism to autonomy can be speeded up.

7. In evaluating Kohlberg's theory, Simpson and Bronfenbrenner believe it is ethnocentric and culturally biased. Rest points out that alternative methods should be used to collect information about moral thinking, rather than relying only on Kohlberg's _____   moral _____ . Simpson faults Kohlberg's   dilemmas idea that getting individuals to reason at a more advanced level will result in corresponding positive changes in their moral behavior.

C. Moral behavior: a social learning view
 1. The study of moral behavior has been influenced primarily by social learning theory. The familiar processes of reinforcement, punishment, and imitation have been invoked to explain how and why children learn certain responses and why their responses differ.
 2. Resistance to temptation and cheating have been the moral behaviors most widely investigated.
 3. There is no reason to expect that a child's behavior will be the same in each realm of moral behavior.
 4. Walter and Harriet Mischel distinguish between the child's _____ _____ ,   moral competence or ability to produce moral behaviors, and his or her _____ _____   moral performance of those behaviors in specific situations.

D. Moral feelings and guilt
  1. Moral feelings have traditionally been assessed
     through measures of _____ .   guilt
  2. Hoffman has been constructing a developmental
     theory of guilt that highlights empathic distress and
     caused attribution.
E. Behaviors that include sharing possessions, contributing
   to worthy causes, and helping people in distress are

   _____ .   altruistic
  1. In general, altruism increases as children develop.
  2. Hoffman's view of altruism emphasizes

     _____ _____ .   person permanence
  3. The level at which empathy is aroused and the speed
     of the altruistic act increases in conjunction with the
     number and intensity of distress cues given by the
     victim.
  4. Role-taking and perspective-taking skills refer to the
     understanding that other people have feelings and
     perceptions different from one's own.
  5. The work of Radke-Yarrow suggests that family
     experiences play a critical part in the development
     of altruistic behavior in children.
F. Moral education
  1. Dewey argued that students learn about obedience
     and defiance of authority rather than about
     democratic principles in the _____   hidden

     _____ .   curriculum
  2. Other educational theorists believe that, while it is
     difficult to specify the appropriate moral virtues to
     instill in children, it is possible to identify generally
     accepted moral virtues and to inform students about
     them.
  3. A group of educational planners led by

     _____ stresses that the moral-   Kohlberg
     reasoning skills of children should be developed.

Exercises

Self-Review

Circle the letter of the best response.

1. When a female child assumes the behaviors characteristic of the female role, she has acquired
   a. self-permanence.
   b. sex-role attitudes.
   c. gender identity.
   d. androgyny.

2. The central construct in Block's research on sex-role development is the
   a. self.
   b. superego.
   c. id.
   d. ego.

3. Gender constancy is acquired during ages
   a. two to six.
   b. three to seven.
   c. four to nine.
   d. five to ten.

4. Kohlberg believes that before children acquire gender constancy they must have attained the
   a. sensori-motor stage.
   b. preoperational stage.
   c. concrete operational stage.
   d. formal operational stage.

5. A submissive parent is not likely to foster
   a. reinforcement.
   b. imitation.
   c. androgyny.
   d. femininity.

6. The social agent most likely to reinforce feminine behavior is a(n)
   a. teacher.
   b. peer.
   c. aunt.
   d. uncle.

7. The theorist who defines a sex-role stereotype as a broad category that reflects our impressions about people is
   a. Hoffman.
   b. Mischel.
   c. Kohlberg.
   d. Piaget.

8. Women are superior to men in
   a. visual ability.
   b. mathematical ability.
   c. verbal ability.
   d. spatial ability.

9. Spence and her colleagues advocate classifying as androgenous those who score
   a. low on the feminine and masculine personality scales.
   b. high on the feminine and low on the masculine personality scales.
   c. low on the feminine and high on the masculine personality scales.
   d. high on both the feminine and masculine personality scales.

10. The theorist who claimed that sexuality is essentially unlearned and instinctual is
    a. Piaget.
    b. Freud.
    c. Hoffman.
    d. Heinz.

11. Which of the following is *false*?
    a. Fathers have no impact on sex-role development of their daughters.
    b. Fathers are more involved in socializing their sons than their daughters.
    c. Female teachers are more likely to reward feminine behavior.
    d. Children reward sex-appropriate play of their peers.

12. The average child watches television
    a. one to two hours a day.
    b. two to four hours a day.
    c. three to five hours a day.
    d. four to seven hours a day.

13. In his research on sex-role development, John Money focuses on
    a. critical periods.
    b. stages.
    c. stereotypes.
    d. socialization.

14. The study of moral behavior has been influenced primarily by
    a. psychoanalytic theory.
    b. ethology.
    c. social learning theory.
    d. humanism.

15. According to Kohlberg, most adolescents are at what level of moral development?
    a. postconventional
    b. concrete
    c. abstract
    d. conventional

16. In Hoffman's view, an early landmark in the development of altruism is
    a. egocentricism.
    b. person permanence.
    c. moral realism.
    d. moral autonomy.

17. When a child learns that other people have different feelings, the child has acquired
    a. perspective-taking skills.
    b. autonomy.
    c. moral realism.
    d. conventional.

18. A concern with imminent justice is characteristic of what stage of moral reasoning?
    a. realism
    b. autonomy
    c. good-boy
    d. conventional

19. How many stages of moral reasoning has Kohlberg proposed?
    a. four
    b. five
    c. six
    d. seven

20. In which stage of moral development will a child consider a person's intent?
    a. moral realism
    b. moral autonomy
    c. concrete operational
    d. formal operational

Comprehension

1. You are a social learning theorist interested in moral development. What would you study? How would the focus of your study differ from that of a cognitive-developmental theorist?

2. Discussions of sex-role development usually center on the influence of parents on their children. However, children are exposed to numerous other social agents. Select one group of social agents and describe its influence on sex-role development.

Application

1. Piaget developed his ideas about moral development by having children make judgments about two stories that focus on two different characters. Following the presentation of each story, the child is asked to decide which character is naughtier, and why. Here is a sample.

   When Mary's mother went shopping, Mary climbed up on a chair to get a cookie from the cookie jar. Mary knew she was not supposed to have cookies before dinner. While she was climbing down from the chair, her foot hit a glass and it broke.

   One day Tina was helping her mother set the dinner table. As she was carrying the water glasses into the dining room, she tripped and the glasses broke.

Present these stories first to three four-year-olds and then to three eight-year-olds. Ask each child which of the two children in these stories was naughtier and why. Record the results below. Do the results correspond to Piaget's description of moral development?

2. Devise a survey to determine how accurately the public differentiates between actual and mythical sex differences. Compile a list of adjectives like that in your text, and ask ten adults of different ages to check the ones they think best describe men in our society. Record the results below. How accurate were your respondents? Which adjectives were checked correctly most often? Which were checked incorrectly most often?

Answers

Self-Review

1. c		11. a	
2. d		12. c	
3. b		13. a	
4. c		14. c	
5. b		15. d	
6. a		16. b	
7. b		17. a	
8. c		18. a	
9. d		19. c	
10. b		20. b	

Comprehension

1. As a social learning theorist, you would study moral behaviors such as altruism, cheating, and resistance to temptation. A cognitive-developmental theorist would study judgments and perceptions.
2. The feedback teachers give boys and girls influence their sex-typed behaviors. Your answer should include discussion of the findings of the Serbin, O'Leary, Kent, and Tonick study (1973) and the review of studies by Beverly Fagot (1973).

14 Problems and Disturbances in Infancy, Childhood, and Adolescence

Objectives

When you have mastered the material in this chapter, you will be able to—

1. discuss the effects of maternal diet, drugs, and emotional state on the newborn;
2. discuss problems and disturbances of infancy;
3. discuss problems and disturbances experienced by elementary school children;
4. discuss problems and disturbances experienced by adolescents;
5. discuss the nature and types of juvenile delinquency.

Key Terms

alcohol
anorexia
anxiety
childhood schizophrenia
compulsions
ecoholalia
embryo
encopesis
enuresis
impulsive delinquent
infantile autism
neurotic disturbances
nightmares

night terrors
obsessions
phobia
psychopathology
psychosis
REM
school phobia
social delinquent
sudden infant death syndrome
symbiotic infantile psychosis
thalidomide
unsocialized delinquent

Synopsis

I. Infancy and Early Childhood
  A. Prenatal development and the birth process
    1. Since the fetus receives all its nutrients from the mother's blood, the mother must have a good, balanced diet if the fetus is to develop normally.
      a) Pregnant women whose diets do not provide adequate nutrients have more premature deliveries; infants with lower birth weights; more complications, such as anemia and toxemia; and prolonged labors.
      b) Research also reveals that too much of certain vitamins may cause problems for the developing _____ .   embryo
    2. Certain drugs ingested by the mother may have an effect on the fetus.
      a) In 1961, a number of babies were born deformed after their mothers had taken the then-popular mild tranquilizer,

         _____ .   Thalidomide
      b) The fetus is also adversely affected when the mother smokes or drinks heavily.
    3. There are several ways in which the mother's emotional state can influence the infant.
      a) During times of stress, the amount of certain hormones in the blood stream increases; the same physical changes that have been stimulated in the mother can appear in the fetus—changes in heart rate, respiration, and blood pressure.
      b) An emotionally distraught mother may have more difficulty with labor that involves irregular contractions.
      c) In one investigation, babies of highly anxious mothers cried more before feedings and were more active than the babies born to less anxious mothers.
  B. Crib death
    1. The unexplained death of a child in the first year of   sudden
       life is referred to as _____   infant death
       _____ _____   syndrome
       _____ .

2. After the first ten days of life, infant crib death is responsible for more deaths in the first year of life than any other cause.

C. Eating problems

1. Excessive weight gain in infancy is linked with a high incidence of obesity at six, seven, and eight years of age.

2. The term given to the refusal to eat, which may vary from children who have fussy appetites to those who endanger their lives with starvation, is

    _____ .   anorexia

D. Sleeping problems

1. Children may vary considerably with regard to their sleep requirements, but parents usually have some preconceived notion of how much sleep their children need.

2. Parental inconsistency, failure to set limits, and reinforcement of behaviors that tend to postpone going to sleep may interfere with sleep.

3. Nightmares are reasonably common among children, occuring during the last third of the night in the stage of sleep called _____ .   REM

E. Elimination problems

1. The involuntary passing of urine in children older than three or four is _____ .   enuresis

2. The elimination problem relating to defecation is

    _____ .   encopresis

F. Infantile autism, childhood schizophrenia, and symbiotic infantile psychosis

1. Infantile autism, often diagnosed during infancy, may persist well into childhood. Probably the most distinguishing characteristic of autistic children is their inability to relate to other people.

   a) Autistic children often have speech problems. Those who do learn to speak may engage in a type of speech called _____ .   echolalia

   b) Autistic children are not flexible in adapting to new routines and changes in their daily life.

   c) Perhaps the most famous treatment program with autistic children is that of Lovaas, who combines behavior modification and operant conditioning, using rewards and punishments in a systematic way to shape the child's linguistic behavior.

d) Another viable method is treating autistic children involves the use of sign language in combination with spoken equivalents and successive approximations in a behavior-modification approach to teaching communication skills.

2. The term childhood schizophrenia is usually not applied to children younger than five years of age.

   a) Mednick views childhood schizophrenia as a pattern of avoidance behavior and an inability to handle stressful situations because of brain damage.

3. A severe abnormality that involves personality disorganization and loss of contact with reality is a _____ .   psychosis

   a) Some experts have suggested that there are two types of psychotic behaviors in children, one stemming from biological predispositions on the part of the child and the other emanating from deficiencies in the child's interactions with his or her social world.

   b) A child who cannot tolerate even a brief separation from his or her mother may have

   _____ _____   symbiotic infantile
   _____ .   psychosis

II. Elementary School Years

  A. Frequent problems reported by elementary school children

    1. Possibly because of the increased conformity to routines and the more noticeable comparisons of children's social and intellectual development, the rate of referrals to mental health clinics increases rapidly in the elementary school years.

    2. Achenbach concluded that the greatest increase in mental health referrals in the elementary school years is school-related.

  B. Neurotic disturbances

    1. Anxieties, phobias, obsessions, compulsions, and depression are the most common of a type of disturbance experienced by children. This type of disturbance is called _____ .   neurotic

2. An unpleasant state that involves the anticipation of something uncomfortable or painful is

_____ . anxiety
3. A strong, unreasonable fear of certain people, objects, or situations is a _____ . phobia
4. Unwanted ideas or fears that intrude into the child's thoughts are _____ . obsessions
5. Repetitive, stereotyped actions called into play to ward off imaginary threats are

_____. compulsions

III. The Adolescent Years
  A. Drug abuse
    1. A White House paper on drug use prepared for the president indicated that slightly more than one of every four adolescents between the ages of twelve and seventeen had tried _____ . marijuana
      a) The National Institute on Drug Abuse reports that when marijuana is used daily in heavy amounts it may impair the human

_____ _____ . reproductive system
      b) The highest usage of marijuana occurred when an adolescent's friends smoke marijuana and his or her parents took drugs (barbiturates and alcohol, for example).
    2. Many parents and other adults do not consider alcohol to be a drug, although it is just that.
      a) The most commonly used and abused psychoactive substance among adolescents in the United States is _____ . alcohol
      b) Alcohol is a depressant that primarily affects the central nervous system.
      c) Investigators have found that adolescents who have drinking problems are more likely to engage in deviant actions and condone transgressions than those who are not problem drinkers.
  B. Juvenile delinquency
    1. The term applied to children and adolescents who break the law or engage in behavior that is considered illegal is _____

_____ . juvenile delinquent

2. Alan Ross describes juvenile delinquency as the failure to develop sufficient behavioral control. The juvenile delinquent may fail to learn the difference between acceptable and unacceptable behavior or to develop adequate control to use the distinction as a guide to behavior.

3. Delinquents may also have developed inadequate standards of conduct, depending on the types of models they experience, and few ego-enhancing competencies.

4. The delinquent who knows that delinquent behavior is wrong and that he or she will probably be punished, but whose poor self-control around attractive stimuli overrides his or her standards of conduct, is called _____ .   impulsive

5. The delinquent who has not developed appropriate internal controls to refrain from engaging in delinquent behavior is called _____ .   unsocialized
It is generally thought that antisocial behavior is produced by deficient socialization on the part of the family.

6. The delinquent who develops control over behavior but who gives in to norms and delinquent standards of the peer group, which are in conflict with those of society at large, is called _____ .   social

7. Attempts to reduce delinquent behavior have not been very successful, as evidenced by its increase in recent years. However, techniques to strengthen positive family and school relationships can foster social competence.

C. Depression
1. Adolescents who show strong indications of depression are often responding to the loss of someone they love.

2. In a recent national survey of depression, it was found that females show higher incidences of depression than males, that black females show markedly high depressive traits, and that depression is more common in lower-income than higher-income families.

3. Some psychologists have speculated that depression has a genetic base, while others argue that the problem is learned.

D. Suicide
    1. Bronfenbrenner cites statistics that show that adolescent suicide attempts have almost tripled since 1955.
    2. In some instances parental problems may be the main factor in a suicide attempt, while in others peer problems may be at the root of the disturbance.
    3. The increase in adolescent suicide during the last twenty-five years is a symptom of the stress that many adolescents now experience as they try to grow from dependent children to independent adults.

IV. The Invulnerables
    A. The most remarkable phenomenon about invulnerable youth is their recovery after stress.
    B. Garmezy says that we need a science of developmental
    _____ .   psychopathology

Exercises

Self-Review

Circle the letter of the best response.

1. Infants who have difficulty relating to others are suspected of being
    a. neurotic.
    b. autistic.
    c. submissive.
    d. nurturant.

2. Speech disturbances often are characteristic of children diagnosed as
    a. popular.
    b. dominant.
    c. schizophrenic.
    d. neurotic.

3. Low birth weight, anemia, and prolonged labor are characteristic of
    a. an anxious parent.
    b. high blood pressure.
    c. hyperactivity.
    d. maternal stress.

4. The neonate's heartbeat can be influenced by
   a. maternal anemia.
   b. the father's occupation.
   c. maternal nutrition.
   d. maternal stress.

5. Active babies have been found to have mothers who are
   a. defensive.
   b. anxious.
   c. withdrawn.
   d. obese.

6. Another name for sudden infant death syndrome is
   a. crib death.
   b. anorexia.
   c. encopresis.
   d. echolalia.

7. Anorexia means that a child refuses to
   a. sleep.
   b. eat.
   c. urinate.
   d. socialize.

8. Parental inconsistency can lead to problems with
   a. health.
   b. school work.
   c. play.
   d. sleeping.

9. What is more likely to occur during the REM portion of sleep?
   a. encopresis
   b. convulsions
   c. enuresis
   d. nightmares

10. Enuresis is thought to be a problem behavior following age
    a. two.
    b. four.
    c. five.
    d. six.

11. A child who is diagnosed as having symbiotic infantile psychosis is characterized by
    a. separation anxiety.
    b. encopresis.
    c. convulsions.
    d. obsessions.

12. The behavior that occurs when a child repeats the same words or phrases over and over is known as
    a. enuresis.
    b. psychosis.
    c. echolalia.
    d. neurosis.

13. Lovaas is best known for his treatment of
    a. retardation.
    b. depression.
    c. drug addiction.
    d. autism.

14. The reproductive system is sometimes affected by the heavy use of
    a. alcohol.
    b. marijuana.
    c. psychoactive substances.
    d. spinach.

15. Alcohol has found to have harmful effects on
    a. the reproductive system.
    b. newborns.
    c. production of enzymes.
    d. muscles.

16. Thalidomide was found to cause
    a. psychosis.
    b. submissiveness.
    c. hyperactivity.
    d. deformities.

17. The mother's blood supplies the baby with
    a. nutrients.
    b. antibodies.
    c. minerals.
    d. strength.

18. The definition of juvenile delinquency is thought to be
    a. too narrow.
    b. too broad.
    c. unnecessary.
    d. irrelevant.

19. The drug most widely used by adolescents is
    a. marijuana.
    b. cocaine.
    c. alcohol.
    d. tobacco.

20. The number of adolescent suicides has
    a. doubled since 1955.
    b. tripled since 1955.
    c. decreased since 1955.
    d. stayed the same since 1955.

Comprehension

1. You are a child development specialist and have been asked by your local PTA to make a presentation on environmental influences on human development. Indicate in detail what information you will include in your lecture.

Application

1. The term juvenile delinquent is applied to children and adolescents who break the law or engage in behavior that is considered illegal. Social workers probably have more day-to-day experience with juvenile delinquents than any other group of professionals. Ask a social worker what he or she thinks are variables that contribute to the development of juvenile delinquency. Also ask the social worker why the rate of juvenile delinquency is rising. Record the responses to your questions.

2. Visit a school or class in your community whose purpose is to educate children with behavioral disorders. Explain to the principal that you are studying a unit on childhood behavior disorders and that you would like to observe children in a behavioral-disorders class. Observe the children for at least twenty minutes. Record your impressions and observations of the children, the instructor, and their interpersonal relationships.

Answers

Self-Review

1.	b	11.	a
2.	c	12.	c
3.	d	13.	d
4.	d	14.	b
5.	b	15.	b
6.	a	16.	d
7.	b	17.	a
8.	d	18.	b
9.	d	19.	c
10.	b	20.	b

Comprehension

1. Drugs, alcohol, the mother's physical health and emotional state.